PRAY. THINK. ACT.

J. AUGUSTINE WETTA, O.S.B.

PRAY. THINK. ACT.

Make Better Decisions with the Desert Fathers

IGNATIUS PRESS   SAN FRANCISCO

Cover art:
Napoleon Crossing the Alps (1801) by Jacques-Louis David
Château de Malmaison. Wikimedia Commons
St. Anthony Abbot and the Centaur (1642) by Francesco Guarino
Photograph courtesy of Sotheby's, 2021

Cover design by J. Augustine Wetta and Enrique J. Aguilar

© 2023 by Ignatius Press, San Francisco
All rights reserved
ISBN 978-1-62164-581-8 (PB)
ISBN 978-1-64229-243-5 (eBook)
Library of Congress Control Number 2022941312
Printed in the United States of America ∞

For Father Paul Chovanec,
who inspired the best decision I ever made

CONTENTS

Acknowledgments   9

Preface   11

Introduction   15
  Who Were the Desert Fathers—and Mothers?   18
  The Structure of This Book   21

Step 1: Pray   25
  Part 1: Retreat   29
  Part 2: Repent   34
  Part 3: Rebuild   39

Step 2: Think   45
  Part 1: Reduce   48
  Part 2: Refer   55
  Part 3: Reflect   61

Step 3: Act   67
  Part 1: Resolve   69
  Part 2: Relax   74
  Part 3: Revisit   79

Conclusion   85

Appendix A: Decision Guide   89

Appendix B: Journal of a Decision   95

Resources   121

Illustration Sources   123

ACKNOWLEDGMENTS

Special thanks to my brother monks and all the great saints who helped me write this book:

Sr. Jacinta, Mother John Mary, Mother Louise Marie, Sr. Mary Michael (who thought up most of the homework assignments in the last book and never got credit for it!), Mother Paschal, and Sr. Anna Marie.

Dr. Brad White, Dan Hill, Br. John Therese, Br. Leo Mary, Fr. Leonard Mary, Fr. Richard Saint Louis, Mrs. Barbara Kruse, Mrs. Julia Masetti, and Mrs. Ann Griesedieck.

Mr. John Addleman, Dr. Tim Flanigan, Mrs. Tamara Cesare, Ms. Emma Ricketts, Mr. Jordan Cherick, Dr. Rob Furey, Mr. Scott Brown, Fr. Rene Pellessier, the

Rempe family, Mr. Kellen Plaxco, Sir Isom Williams, Ms. Marly Youmans, and Mrs. Ann Brannan.

Mr. Dennis Toscano, Mr. Stausch Boyle, Mr. Derek Colins, Mr. Lamar Latimore, Mrs. Lauren White, Mr. Brent Decker, Mr. Mike Nickolai, Fr. Chris Martin, Fr. Derek Lappe, Mr. Victor Masetti, Mr. Matt Abide, Dr. Andy Reyes, Fr. Mark Goring, Fr. Fadi Auro, and Fr. Noah Waldman.

Mr. Umar Lee, Mrs. Carrie Lane, Mr. Jon-Pierre Mitchom, Mr. Chris Fisher, Mr. Frank Wetta, Mrs. Jean Wetta, Dr. Tim Kalhorn, Fr. Patrick Nwokoye, Mr. Ron Huelsmann, Fr. Mark Mary, Fr. John Paul Mary, Dr. James J. O'Donnell, Bishop Edward Rice, and Sir Basil Damukaitis.

Ms. Dee Webb, Ms. Dawn Eden Goldstein, Mrs. Lauren Fisher, Godmother Tina Stretch, Abbot Lawrence Stasyszen, Sr. Markina Finlay, Fr. Gregory Pine, and Fr. Bryce Sibley.

Monika, Nick, and Marek Parafiniuk; Rachel, Mary, Jessica, and Georgia Decker.

Fr. Paul Chovanec and "Biker" Bob Trump.

And my entire family at the Saint Louis Priory School.

PREFACE

The Road Not Taken

Two roads diverged in a yellow wood,
And sorry I could not travel both
And be one traveler, long I stood
And looked down one as far as I could
To where it bent in the undergrowth;

Then took the other, as just as fair,
And having perhaps the better claim,
Because it was grassy and wanted wear;
Though as for that the passing there
Had worn them really about the same,

And both that morning equally lay
In leaves no step had trodden black.
Oh, I kept the first for another day!
Yet knowing how way leads on to way,
I doubted if I should ever come back.

I shall be telling this with a sigh
Somewhere ages and ages hence:
Two roads diverged in a wood, and I—
I took the one less traveled by,
And that has made all the difference.[1]

What does this poem by Robert Frost mean to you? Does it conjure up images of courage and independence? Do you imagine that "the traveler" is a smart, self-sufficient go-getter who takes the more difficult path in life and expects some day to look back with satisfaction on a life well lived? If so, you're wrong. But don't feel bad; just about everyone reads this poem the wrong way. It turns out, the whole point of the poem is that the speaker took the road less traveled by and all it did was make his life harder, because both roads ended in the same place.

I don't know if Robert Frost ever read the Desert Fathers, but he certainly lived like one, and his poem neatly surmises (albeit in a uniquely American way) what those early monks were trying to say. The

[1] Robert Frost, "The Road Not Taken", Poetry Foundation, https://www.poetryfoundation.org/poems/44272/the-road-not -taken.

very first sentence of the *Apophthegmata Patrum* (*The Sayings of the Desert Fathers*) reads: "These sayings of the holy fathers are recorded in this book to school those of you who want to pursue the heavenly way of life and are willing to travel the road to the kingdom of heaven by following in their footsteps." In other words, the Desert Fathers will guide you along the road well taken—whether and how many other people choose to travel this way is irrelevant. Follow their advice, and you won't have to look back on your life with a sigh and make up some platitude to explain why it was so hard. "Thus says the LORD: 'Stand by the roads, and look, and ask for the ancient paths, where the good way is; and walk in it, and find rest for your souls'" (Jer 6:16). Sometimes the road not taken is not taken for a good reason.

INTRODUCTION

A certain monk named Serapion was given a Gospel man-uscript, but he only read as far as the words "Sell what you have and give to the poor" because he immediately sold it and gave the money to the poor.

My friend Egbert has a whole new attitude. He loves himself because he understands that he is made in the image and likeness of God. If his friends ignore him, it doesn't bother him anymore because he recognizes that God loves him; he doesn't need to be sure everyone else does. As a sign

of his new attitude, Egbert changed his name to Paphnutius. It seemed to suit him for a time, but then he
began to wonder whether that was such a great idea.
Paphnutius is kind of an odd name, so he changed it
back to Egbert. But his friends protested that the new
name better suited his personality; so he changed it
back again. Now he's wondering if he did all that just
to please his friends, and he thinks maybe he should
scrap both names in favor of Mungo.[1]

You see, Egbert has a new problem that is, I think,
increasingly common: he can't make up his mind. And
his new name is just the beginning. There are bigger
decisions on the horizon—issues like marriage and
vocation, for example—but he may never have time to
consider those because he can't even decide what he's
having for dinner. When he does decide, he spends the
rest of the meal wondering if he made the right choice.
And this is no way to live. After all, Jesus himself said,
"No one who puts his hand to the plow and looks back
is fit for the kingdom of God" (Lk 9:62).

Luckily, monks have a solution to this problem of
indecision. In his *Rule for Monasteries*, Saint Benedict
called it "the school of the Lord's service". But it's
older, even, than the *Rule*. It goes all the way back
to the Egypt of Late Antiquity and the very first men
and women who left the chaotic world of the falling
Roman Empire to pursue lives of silent contemplation
in the desert. These Desert Fathers and Mothers had

[1] These are all real saints' names, in case you were wondering.

their faults, to be sure; but they had one virtue in their favor: they were wholehearted. Like Serapion, they tended to see the world in very clear terms; and once they knew what they were doing, they did it. They refused to water down the Gospel message. They put their hand to the plow and never looked back—well, almost never.

Who Were the Desert Fathers— and Mothers?

Father Poemen said, "A monk is truly a monk when he has hard choices to make."

The very first monks and nuns began to appear in the Egyptian desert around the second half of the third century A.D. They wanted to be martyrs, but they had a problem: the Roman Empire at the time was sympathetic to Christianity. In fact, Christianity was made the official religion of the whole empire in A.D. 380, so there were precious few opportunities to be flayed, burned, or eaten by lions. Instead, they opted for what they called "white martyrdom"—a form of extreme Christianity that took literally the scriptural

commands to "be perfect" (Mt 5:48), to "pray constantly" (1 Thess 5:17), and to "sell what you possess
and give to the poor" (Mt 19:21). They considered
themselves spiritual athletes—*athletae Dei*—and they
competed with one another in fasting, abstinence,
poverty, asceticism, and even humility. As plagues
and wars and political chaos began to overwhelm the
civilized world, more young men and women began
to see the folly of it all, and the desert began to fill up
with monks and nuns. Like Jesus, they were deeply
hesitant to write anything down, but also like Jesus,
they were happy to give advice when asked, because
all that meditation and silence had the effect of making them master problem solvers. Visitors began to
address them as Father and Mother (*Abba* and *Amma*
in Aramaic). And their advice was passed down from
monk to monk for hundreds of years.

Monks still tell one another these stories, and many
of them have to do with decision-making. But here's
the catch: a good monk will always prefer listening over
talking, so even when asked a question, an old monk is
likely to pose a question in return. Or he might tell one
of these stories and let you figure out how it applies.
This is wiser than it sounds, because anyone who is
good at making decisions has made enough bad ones
to understand his own frailty, has enough experience to
understand the context, and has enough common sense
to avoid making someone else's decision for him.

Nonetheless, as Paphnutius begins the process of
making his decision, there are a few questions he

should ask himself, and a few techniques he can use to clarify the issue at hand. In this book, each section will start with a story from the lives of the Desert Fathers. These stories were told to me by old monks, and every monk puts his own spin on them. Whenever possible, I've tried not to look them up, but simply to retell them the way they were told to me. For a complete collection of the stories the way they were actually written down, see the *Apophthegmata Patrum Aegyptiorum* of Hieronymus Palladius. Or if your Latin, Greek, and Coptic are a little rusty, any book by Benedicta Ward will do.

The Structure of This Book

Father Paphnutius said, "There are three ways to embrace a vocation, and they are all essential to discernment, no matter what sort of life you choose. The first comes from God, the second from man, and the third from necessity. In the first case, God speaks directly to the human heart. In the second case, the advice and virtues of some mortal stir the heart. The third way is imposed upon you, for you have made the wrong decision and are therefore put to the test. You turn toward God by necessity."

Even a cursory survey of the latest psychological, sociological, economic, and philosophical books on decision-making will make one thing very clear: the experts can't decide how to go about it. Are there four stages? Five stages? Six? Seven? Eight? Is it even possible to make a decision?

Psychologists seem to think there are five stages (clarify your goals, generate options, search for information, consider the effects, and implement the plan);[2] doctors seem to prefer six (define the problem, establish criteria, consider the alternatives, choose the best one, develop a plan, and evaluate the outcome);[3] while ethicists claim there are eight (create a community, acknowledge the problem, consider different interpretations, make a judgment, look for fallacies, act, reflect on that action, and ... well ... reflect on it again).[4] Each is useful in its own way, and I encourage you to spend some time looking them over.[5] However, all these folks could have saved themselves a lot of trouble if they had taken a look at what Paphnutius had to say back in A.D. 325.

I would like to offer his three "ways" as the blueprint for making any decision, and so, with the help of other ancient Desert Fathers, I've come up with the

[2] Leon Mann, Ros Harmoni, Colin Power, Gery Beswick, and Cheryl Ormond, "Effectiveness of the GOFER Course in Decision Making for High School Students", *Journal of Behavioral Decision Making* 1, no. 3 (July 1988): 159–68.

[3] Kristina L. Guo, "DECIDE: A Decision-Making Model for More Effective Decision Making by Health Care Managers", *The Health Care Manager* 39, no. 3 (June 2008): 133–41.

[4] John Pijanowski, "The Role of Learning Theory in Building Effective College Ethics Curricula", *Journal of College and Character* 10, no. 3 (February 2009): 1–13.

[5] Believe it or not, Wikipedia is pretty good on this. Just look up "decision-making", but be sure to go read the sources for yourself, because each strategy has its own clinical, scientific, and professional jargon, and it is sometimes hard to distinguish between that and ideology. What's more, the exact number of stages varies depending on exactly whom you ask.

following three steps, each divided into three parts, followed by some "dos and don'ts".

The first thing you have to do is pray, withdrawing from the world and reflecting on your shortcomings, emptying yourself so as to hear, as clearly as possible, God's take on the situation. Second, you have to simplify the question as much as possible, collect advice, and consider all the possible influences and outcomes. But eventually, you have to act, taking everything you've learned and committing to a particular choice, while allowing for the possibility that you may have made a mistake. Then you leave it in God's hands.

In other words,

1. PRAY
    Retreat
    Repent
    Rebuild
2. THINK
    Reduce
    Refer
    Reflect
3. ACT
    Resolve
    Relax
    Revisit

At the end of this book, you will find two appendices. Because I am a teacher, I can't resist giving homework. So appendix A, "Decision Guide", has some worksheets for you to use the next time you need to make a big decision. Don't worry, it won't be graded. There are no wrong answers, and you can use any kind of writing utensil you like. But no cheating! This is your decision, and yours alone. Don't let someone else make the decision for you.

Probably the question I get asked the most is: "How did you decide to become a monk?" I admit that this is an unusual decision, but it happens to be the best one I ever made. To show how I made it, I put together appendix B, "Journal of a Decision", which includes excerpts from my diaries going all the way back to my senior year of high school, when I first consciously started to engage in the long, exhilarating, clumsy process of discerning my vocation. I cleaned up some of the grammar, but I otherwise left my entries pretty much the way I found them—with dead ends, missteps, shifting landscapes, raw emotions, and all. To be sure, everyone comes to his vocation in a unique way; but I hope you'll see some of yourself in my experiences and find in me a companion for the journey.

STEP 1: PRAY

Three friends decided to become saints, and they weren't afraid to put in the work necessary to do so. The first chose to spend his life reconciling enemies. The second chose to work with the sick. The third went into the desert to live in silence and prayer. Now, in spite of all his hard work, the first could not make peace in the world; so he decided to find the one who was serving the sick. He found his friend discouraged and overworked as well. Together, they set out to find the one who was dwelling in the desert.

They found him living quite peacefully and begged him to tell them what had gone wrong with their own efforts. After a short silence, he poured some water into a bowl and said to them, "Bring me some mud." They each went outside his cell, picked up a handful of mud, and, upon his instruction, threw it into the bowl.

"What do you see?" asked the monk.

"We see a bowl of muddy water."

He waited a bit, then asked them again, "What do you see?"

Again, they answered, "A bowl of muddy water."

"Give it time," he said, and went off to bed, leaving them staring into the bowl of mud.

The next morning, after the sun had risen, he returned and asked them, "Now what do you see?"

"Ah! Now we understand," they said, for they could see their own reflections.

Then the monk said to them, "It is the same for those who live among noise and distraction. A man must first be still enough to see himself clearly. Only then can he be of service to others."

Before you can decide anything, you need to calm down and quiet your mind. It is almost impossible to make a good decision while you are upset or distracted. And even then, it can be hard to distinguish between distraction and inspiration.

Many years ago, I was asked to give a Confirmation retreat in Bowling Green, Missouri. I'd done it once or twice before, so I thought I knew what I was getting myself into. But when I arrived, it turned out that the entire Bowling Green High School football team had decided to get confirmed that year. These

enormous, corn-fed Missouri boys weren't a bit inter-
ested in what the "cool monk" had to say.

I decided to make it a silent retreat.

Ironically, I stumbled into success when I said to
them, "I don't know if you guys can handle this, but
we're going to try some silent prayer now." Appar-
ently, it was my lack of confidence in them that caught
their attention. They wanted to know why I thought
they "couldn't handle" it. They saw it as a challenge.
So we did five minutes of silent meditation, then fif-
teen, then thirty. They started to compete with one
another to see who could be the quietest. I've never
seen anything like it. This one lineman—he was
maybe six foot five—was focusing so hard, he actually grunted and flexed during his prayer. I couldn't
believe it. At the end of the day, they decided to go for
forty-five minutes. I had no sooner rung the bell than
I realized I had forgotten to tell them about the rosary,
the Jesus prayer, the difficulties and dangers of silent
meditation, the need for a spiritual guide, the gifts of
the Holy Spirit ... Before I knew it, the time was up,
and I hadn't even started praying.

I gathered all the guys together and decided that
this was at least an opportunity to share with them my
own experience of weakness and distraction. "Fellas,"
I said, "I have to admit, I didn't even start praying this
time around. All I could think of was the stuff I'd forgotten to tell you."

For the first time that day, the lineman (whom I had
nicknamed Flex) raised his hand. "Father," he said,

"how do you know that wasn't Jesus trying to help you run the retreat?" I looked around at the others, and they were all nodding like a bunch of old monks. I began to wonder if I shouldn't have let Flex run the retreat. I mean, here was I, so preoccupied with teaching folks to listen to God, that I'd missed it when he actually spoke to me!

My point is this: Don't let the technique get in the way of actually listening. Take time to waste time with God, and the answer may just come to you without any work at all. "If any of you lacks wisdom," wrote the apostle James, "let him ask God, who gives to all men generously and without reproach, and it will be given him" (Jas 1:5). Remember that you will have to be listening. God rarely shouts anyone down.

Part 1: Retreat

Father Elias said, "An old monk was tempted by demons, who bothered him day and night. One night, a demon beat him up and dragged him out of his cell by the hair. The brother cried out, 'Jesus, save me.' And immediately the demon ran away. When the old monk began to weep in gratitude, the Lord said to him, 'Why didn't you call sooner?' "

You've read the book/seen the movie/heard the story a thousand times: the hero goes looking for a treasure only to find ... it was with him all along! There's a reason this plot twist has become such a cliché: there's truth in it. Often you will find that the solution to this or that problem was obvious from the start—you just never slowed down long enough to see it.

I remember telling my novice master, "As much time as I've spent in prayer, you would think that I'd have more faith now than ever. But instead, I have more doubts and questions."

To which he responded, "You really should pray more."

I must have done a pretty poor job of hiding my frustration, because later that day, I found a note slipped under the door of my cell. On it was written a quote from the Austrian poet Rainer Maria Rilke:

> I would like to beg you, dear Sir ... to have patience with everything unresolved in your heart and to try to love the questions themselves as if they were locked rooms or books written in a very foreign language. Don't search for the answers, which could not be given to you now, because you would not be able to live them. The point is to live everything. Live the questions now. Perhaps then, someday far in the future, you will gradually, without even noticing it, live your way into the answer.[1]

Saint Paul put it a slightly different way: "Have no anxiety about anything," he wrote to the Philippians, "but in everything by prayer and supplication with thanksgiving let your requests be made known to God" (Phil 4:6). Some decisions require deep reflection, some you can't see coming, and others simply cannot be made at all. But no matter what choice lies before you, don't get so caught up in making the

[1] Franz Xaver Kappus and Rainer Maria Rilke, *Letters to a Young Poet* (Novato, CA: New World Library, 2010), 35.

decision that you forget to bring Jesus into it. After all, there are many things you might choose to do "in the heat of the moment" that you would never have done if you had prayed first—and many options you might never have imagined if you hadn't.

on't make a decision while you are high on emotion.

The Devil appeared to a brother disguised as an angel of light and said to him, "I am Gabriel and I have been sent to you."

"I'm just a monk," the brother replied, "Are you sure you weren't supposed to appear to someone else?"

And immediately the Devil vanished.

There's wisdom in what your mom told you: "When you're upset, breathe deeply and count to ten."[2] Not only is it important to let the emotion pass, but if you wait, the situation itself may change, or you may be able to witness a slow development in a particular direction. The Desert Fathers were smart enough to know that their life wasn't for everyone; but they had seen enough young monks come and go to know that

[2] Mom, Yours.

a little time spent in detached reflection would pay off in time saved later on.

Saint Ignatius of Loyola claimed that the ideal state of mind for making a decision was "indifference", but he didn't mean by this that you shouldn't care. He just meant that you should wait until the anger (or infatuation or enthusiasm) passes before making a decision you might regret. This principle applies just as much to when you are elated or depressed as to when you are upset. The monk in the story above was detached enough to question his miraculous vision—and it saved his vocation.

o rethink your decision in different terms.

An old monk used to greet his novices by saying, "May fear, humiliation, hunger, and sorrow be with you."

It may help to reconsider your decision from a different perspective. I have a friend who studied under a famous artist in graduate school. For two years, her mentor made her copy all the old masters *upside down*. In this way, my friend learned to consider each work of art in terms of color and composition rather than being distracted by the subject matter.

A similar approach can be useful when it comes to making a difficult decision. Try widening your options. Then narrow them. Consider the worst—and best— possible outcomes. Ask yourself what you would do if none of these options were possible. The old monk in the passage above wasn't cursing his novices, but trying to get them to reconsider their decisions upside down, that is, in light of a dramatically different set of priorities; because the long-term gains of being humiliated and hungry far outweigh the short-term cost to one's pride and comfort.

Part 2: Repent

A young monk asked an elder, "Father, I keep coming back here day after day. Why should I bother when I still commit the same sins? I am utterly unclean." Now, there were two oil jars in the room, so the old monk said to him, "Before you leave, go and empty out the jar on the left, clean it, and refill it with oil."

He did as he was told.

"I've changed my mind. Empty it out again and clean it."

Again, the young monk complied.

He changed his mind several times, and each time, the young monk cleaned out the jar and refilled it with oil.

"Now," said the old man, "bring me both jars. Which is cleaner?"

Any addict will tell you that one bad choice leads to another. If you don't do something to break the cycle, you wind up constructing a delusory world for yourself that merely encourages more and more self-destructive behavior.[3] As hard as you work, your efforts never seem to pay off, and eventually, you become too exhausted to care.

In monastic circles, we sometimes refer to this exhaustion as "the noonday devil".[4] The monk says to himself (right around noon, when the sun is hot and the work is boring), "I do my prayers. I haven't murdered anyone. I'm basically okay. And it's such hard work fighting this or that vice. What's the point?" The Desert Fathers had a name for this as well; they called it *acedia*—"weakness" in Greek. As a precaution against this, Saint Benedict insisted that his monks take a special vow never to stop repenting. We call this vow *conversatio morum*, literally "change of way". Only constant conversion can keep you from slipping into this uniquely comfortable form of mediocrity.

You might think of it this way: A kid may say to himself, "Why bother brushing my teeth? I'm just going to get food all over them anyway." But everyone knows that if he doesn't regularly brush his teeth, eventually they will rot. So it is with the soul. Regular confession brushes the sin away. If you let the bad

[3] When you get a chance, have a look sometime at the twelve steps of Alcoholics Anonymous. Steps 4–11 are all about confession and atonement.

[4] There's a great book on this topic by Dom Jean-Charles Nault, the abbot of Fontenelle Abbey: *The Noonday Devil: Acedia, the Unnamed Evil of Our Times*, trans. Michael J. Miller (San Francisco: Ignatius Press, 2015). It's well worth your time.

decisions build up, the rot of vice inevitably sets in, and then you're in serious trouble, because vice is a breeding ground for bad decisions; it clouds the judgment and predisposes the soul to choosing alternatives that are not in its best interest.

Conversely, if you keep repenting, your vices will slowly weaken, and virtues will begin to grow in their place. This takes time and endurance, and if you have to repent of the same sin seventy times seven times, you can be assured of forgiveness. What's more, you will begin to acquire a certain clarity of vision that will allow you to see temptation coming and head it off before it strikes. "Draw near to God and he will draw near to you," says Saint James. "Cleanse your hands, you sinners, and purify your hearts, you men of double mind" (Jas 4:8).

on't give up.

A certain brother came to an old monk and said, "What should I do? Every time I start to pray, my thoughts wander off, and I say to myself, 'What's the point? I'm not getting anything out of this.'"

The old monk said to him, "Go back to your cell and stay there. For just as a young calf always returns to its mother, so your spirit will settle down eventually. If, however, you get up and go chasing after your thoughts, you will lose both body and soul."

It often seems, especially in the pursuit of holiness, that we are making little or no progress. We make the same bad choices over and over. Again and again, we return to the Lord with the same sins. This is discouraging—and rightly so—but it doesn't mean we're not making progress. And really, what is the alternative? As the elder pointed out in the story above, to stop repenting would be to lose the soul altogether. In addition to keeping us humble, perseverance demonstrates to God and to ourselves that we have not abandoned hope.

o make up your mind eventually.

An old monk said, "Every morning when the sun rises, I ask myself, 'How shall I do God's will today?' Every evening as the sun sets, I ask myself, 'Did I do it?' "

It's good to have options, but overthinking a decision can be just as bad as having no options at all. Experts call this "analysis paralysis", but I like to call it "the Hamlet effect". As much as I love it, and as many times as I've seen it, about two-thirds of the way through

Shakespeare's longest play, I am strongly tempted to stand up and shout, "I don't care whom you kill, Hamlet, just DO SOMETHING!" Hamlet makes himself, the audience, and everyone around him suffer because he just won't make up his mind. You see, the goal of decision-making isn't to come up with a really good method of decision-making; the goal is *to make the decision*. If, at the end of the day, you've spent so much time on the process that you never got any closer to a conclusion, you can hardly consider the day well spent. Don't get so caught up in collecting information, analyzing data, consulting authorities, and coming up with a plan of action ... that you never act.

Part 3: Rebuild

An old monk said to a brother, "The Devil is the enemy and you are a house. The enemy never stops throwing evil into your house. It is your job to keep throwing it out again. If you neglect this, the house will be so full of evil that you'll no longer be able to get inside. So just keep throwing the evil out, and little by little, by the grace of God, your house will become clean again."

Interestingly, studies show that disciplined people who consistently make wise choices don't have that much more wisdom and self-control than the rest of us.[5] In fact, they may actually have less. Their secret is that they rebuild their environment to encourage

[5] Check out a great book by Charles Duhigg called *The Power of Habit: Why We Do What We Do in Life and Business* (New York: Random House Trade Paperbacks, 2014). It's not a religious book, but the principles translate nicely.

good decisions. For example, if you want to eat more vegetables, just put the veggies in the front of the fridge so that you have to reach over them to get to the cake. Or better yet, throw the cake out altogether (and mix it with the coffee grounds so that you aren't tempted to go dumpster diving). The point of "cleaning out your house" is to create a context for a good decision while you are in a good frame of mind. This way, virtue simply becomes a way of life. If your house (metaphorical and literal) is full of temptations, what chance do you really have to make the right choices?

The good news is that if you make the right choice often enough, it becomes a habit. This is basic virtue theory. Back in the fourth century B.C., Aristotle figured out that if you want to be a good person, you have to practice being good. The soldier doesn't start off brave. He acts as though he's brave over and over until he realizes one day that he actually is what he has longed to be. This is the philosophy behind "fake it till you make it", and it's backed up by some real science. Psychologists found that if they asked folks to hold a pencil in their mouth (which forced a "smile") while they did a difficult task, they actually found the task easier. Other studies show that sitting up straight improves self-confidence; hugging yourself reduces pain; breathing slowly reduces stress; and leaning toward something makes you less afraid of it.[6]

---

[6] F. Marmolejo-Ramos, A. Murata, K. Sasaki, Y. Yamada, A. Ikeda, J.A. Hinojosa, K. Watanabe, M. Parzuchowski, C. Tirado, and R.

Saint Francis de Sales cast this in a more spiritual light when he said, "We learn to study by studying, to play on the lute by playing, to dance by dancing, to swim by swimming. So also we learn to love God and our neighbour by *loving* them, and those who attempt any other method are mistaken."[7] I would add that you learn to make good decisions by making good decisions. So if you are not the sort of person who makes good decisions, "rebuild" yourself in the image of someone who does by making lots of smaller decisions in the right way.

on't rely exclusively on reason.

An elder said, "The pig always does what is in his nature. Sadly, man can stoop even lower."

I had a suitemate in college who worked in the cafeteria. He was always bringing back leftovers. One night, he returned from work with an entire sheet of

Ospina, "Your Face and Moves Seem Happier When I Smile. Facial Action Influences the Perception of Emotional Faces and Biological Motion Stimuli", *Experimental Psychology* 67, no. 1 (2020): 14–22.

[7] Quoted by Jean Pierre Camus in *The Spirit of St. Francis de Sales* (Middlesex: Echo Library, 2007), 41.

red velvet cake two layers thick, five feet by five feet square, with cream cheese icing. My other roommates and I had a rugby game the next morning, and we all knew we shouldn't eat it, but I concocted the following theory based on my very limited understanding of evolutionary biology: a creature would not evolve to eat food that would kill it; therefore, since humans are at the top of the evolutionary scale, the better it tastes, the better it must be for us! Everyone complimented me on my revolutionary genius, and we ate until we were sick. Needless to say, we lost the rugby game the next day. And what did I prove that weekend? Only that it is a silly thing to rely too heavily on your sense of reason, because if you really want to do something, you can find a way to rationalize it.

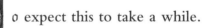 o expect this to take a while.

An elder said, "It takes great toil to change a bad habit. But what is the alternative?"

We are surrounded by promises of easy solutions to complex problems: "Eat all you want and never gain weight!" "Learn a language while you sleep!" "Make money online now!" ... Thus, it can be tempting to think that there might be some sort of algorithm for making good decisions—a hotline you can call or an app you can use that will make up your mind for you. The truth is, every real decision is a sum of your past decisions together with costly (and sometimes heart-breaking) resolutions. "When you come to serve the Lord, prepare yourself for trials," wrote the scribe Ben Sira. "Set your heart right and be steadfast, incline your ear, and receive words of understanding, and do not be hasty in time of calamity" (Sir 2:12).

STEP 2: THINK

A brother said to Father Joseph of Panephysis, "I am at peace in my monastery, but I also feel the call to be a hermit. What should I do?"

The old monk said, "If it is a choice between two options, both of which will bring you peace, place each as it were into a scale. Add to them other thoughts, both encouraging and discouraging. Then weigh them one against the other."

$\mathcal{M}$any people believe that Benjamin Franklin invented the pros and cons list. He himself called it "moral algebra":

When I have thus got [all the pros and cons] together in one view, I endeavour to estimate their respective weights; and where I find two, one on each side, that seem equal, I strike them both out: If I find a reason Pro equal to some two reasons Con, I strike out the three. If I judge some two reasons Con equal to some three reasons Pro, I strike out the five; and thus proceeding I find at length where the balance lies; and if after a day or two of farther consideration nothing new that is of importance occurs on either side, I come to a determination accordingly.[1]

How clever of Franklin to have invented a way to make decisions! But Father Joseph thought of it first. So how is it that a man who was smart enough to discover electricity[2] wasn't wise enough to consult his elders? Because when it comes to decision-making, it can be very easy to fall into a form of chronological snobbery. We assume that just because the advice is old, or from an old person, it doesn't really apply to our current dilemmas. We forget, however, that all old people are, without exception, former young people.

This is very hard to envision, and so we ignore their advice and find ourselves reinventing the wheel.

[1] "From Benjamin Franklin to Joseph Priestly, 19 September 1772", Founders Online, National Archives, accessed February 22, 2022, https://founders.archives.gov/documents/Franklin/01-19-02-0200. (Original source: *The Papers of Benjamin Franklin*, vol. 19, *January 1 through December 31, 1772*, ed. William B. Willcox [New Haven and London: Yale University Press, New Haven and London, 1975], 299–300).

[2] Actually, he didn't do that either. Thales of Miletus was already writing about electricity in the sixth century B.C. He noticed that if you rub a piece of amber (*electron* in Greek) with a cloth, you get sparks.

Consider, for example, the huge number of young people who think it's okay to sleep around before they get married. Thousands of years of tradition and every world religion frown upon this. Yet time and again, this advice is ignored. In theory at least, the sixth commandment could be wrong. But it seems to me that rules like this come about not only through divine revelation, but also through trial and error. So before you arrive at a life-changing conclusion, be sure that you clarify the question, think deeply, weigh your alternatives, and consult the experts ... but do stop to consider the very likely possibility that your elders may have already found an answer.

Part 1: Reduce

A brother asked an old monk, "What shall I do, for the temptations that war against me are many, and I do not know how to fight against them?"

The old man said to him, "This is one demon with many heads. Do not try to fight them all at once. Attack one head, and the others will bleed out."

It can be a great temptation to think you must solve all your problems at once—or that one grand solution will solve them all. But the opposite is true: when you disentangle your decisions, the answers become clearer. Remember the Gospel story of the man born blind? Personally, I am convinced that he was a teenager—and not a very pleasant one. In the course of the story, he shows himself to be lazy, obstinate, disobedient, disrespectful, ungrateful, and irreverent. Interrogated by the authorities concerning his miraculous cure, he answers, "I have told you already, and you would not listen.... Do you too want to become his disciples?" (Jn 9:27) Everything this kid says is dripping with sarcasm. Even Jesus seems to be annoyed by him. But this fellow has one redeeming quality—"redeeming" in the theological sense of the word. He may be disrespectful and obstinate, but *he sticks to the facts*.

"How did you get your sight back?" they ask him.

"I dunno. He stuck mud in my eyes and now I see."

"But that man is a sinner."

"Maybe so. I dunno. I was blind and now I can see."

"But we have no idea where this guy is from."

"Who cares? I was blind and now I can see! How many times do I have to tell you?"

Notice that he makes no profession of faith. And only after relentless interrogation does he finally acknowledge that this man Jesus (whoever he is) must be from God. He doesn't even thank Jesus afterward. Jesus has to find him.

"Do you believe in the Son of Man?" Jesus asks him.

"Who's that?"

"You're talking to him!" Jesus answers.

Saint John tells us that the young man then responds with "I do believe, Lord" and *worshipping Jesus*.

But imagine an alternative ending to this story where the teenager says, "Oh. Right. Thanks a lot for everything, man. But you know, maybe it wasn't you who actually healed me. Maybe that was just a coincidence. Maybe my blindness was all psychological to begin with. Maybe there was something in the mud you put on my eyes. Maybe I'd better go think about this for a while before I make any rash decisions."

I once asked my novice master how I was supposed to know if God was really calling me to be a monk of Saint Louis Abbey.

"Well," he said after some thought, "you're not somewhere else."

Often, when you reduce a question to its most basic elements, the answer becomes obvious.

on't try to predict the outcome.

A monk was tempted to leave his monastery. So, every day, he packed up his stuff and said to himself, "I will leave tomorrow." He did this for nine years, after which, God removed the temptation.

Every decision has one infinitely complex element called "the future". Anything could happen between now and the very next moment: you could win the lottery, slip on a banana peel, be struck by a meteorite[3]

---

[3] Granted, the odds are very slim that you will be hit by a meteorite (about 1 in 700 million). But it happened in Sylacauga, Alabama, in 1954, when a space rock crashed through Ann Hodges' roof, bounced off her radio, and hit her in the thigh. Who knows what her plans were for that evening, but you can bet they didn't include that!

... and because the options are almost infinite, the future is correspondingly hard to predict.

In 2005, Philip Tetlock, a psychologist at the University of Pennsylvania, completed a twenty-year study of predictions. He interviewed nearly three hundred pundits, experts, and hotshots of various types who made a living offering people advice on political trends. He asked them to predict the odds that certain events would occur in the near future: Would so-and-so get elected? Would the economy take a dive? Would war break out in such-and-such a place? By the time he was done, he had compiled over eighty thousand predictions by the world's most knowledgeable and influential experts.

> The results were devastating. The experts performed worse than they would have if they had simply assigned equal probabilities to each of the three potential outcomes. In other words, people who spend their time, and earn their living, studying a particular topic produce poorer predictions than dart-throwing monkeys who would have distributed their choices evenly over the options. Even in the region they knew best, experts were not significantly better than non-specialists.[4]

I've spent a great part of my life making my own predictions: what the next great disaster will be, what

[4] Daniel Kahneman, *Thinking, Fast and Slow* (New York: Farrar, Straus and Giroux, 2013), 219.

will happen if so-and-so gets elected, what will happen if the world overheats or overcools or runs out of frogs, what will happen to my senior theology students if they don't start turning in their blasted homework ... and none of this makes me feel any better. Yet I keep making predictions, because "in these uncertain times" making confident predictions about the future calms me. Admittedly, the calm doesn't last long. I know deep down that human predictions are about as dependable as dart-throwing monkeys—and perhaps more dangerous.

o focus on the positive.

There was a brother who often fell victim to lustful thoughts. Nonetheless, he was determined to stick to his vocation, saying to himself, "Don't you dare abandon the monastic habit." Then he would pray to God in these words: "Lord, you can see I'm no good at this, so restrain me. Save me, Lord, whether I want it or not. I am nothing, but you (being God Almighty and all that) can just force me to be good, can't you? After all, if you had mercy only on the righteous, well, that's not hard to do, is it? And if you saved only the pure, big deal! They were worthy of you to begin with. But to me, unworthy as

I am, perform this mercy, show your loving kindness, for the life of the poor is in your hands." He would pray like this every day, whether he was tempted or not.

On one occasion when he was being tempted, he began night prayer. The Devil could hardly believe what he was seeing. He appeared to the young monk and said, "How is it that you can utter the name of God without blushing all over?"

The brother answered, "This cell is a forge. So, go ahead and hit me with your hammer. You will find that for every blow I receive, you will get one right back. I'm going to keep this up until I die. And I will not stop praying until you stop tempting me. So bring it on! Let's see who wins out in the end—you or God!"

When the demon heard this, he said to him, "You win. If I keep this up, you may even become a saint." And he never bothered that monk again.

If the Devil can't get you to do the wrong thing, he'll get you to worry about not doing the wrong thing; because either way, you're focused on the wrong thing. So think carefully and plan carefully, but understand that worrying about a decision is both ineffective and counterproductive. It focuses on the negative side of the decision—what you're sacrificing or what you're trying to avoid. This is different from analyzing costs and risks because it neglects the one element essential in all decision-making: trust in God. You certainly will make some bad decisions from time to time, and it is inevitable that

53

sometimes you will do the wrong thing. But if whatever you do, you do in the name of Jesus, then, as Saint Ignatius of Loyola said, "God will not be outdone in generosity."

Part 2: Refer

An old monk said, "The prophets wrote books, then came our Fathers, who put them into practice. Those who came after them learned them by heart. Then came the present generation, who wrote them out, put them on shelves, and never looked at them again."

Once you are in the right frame of mind, have thought deeply about the decision itself, made lists of pros and cons, pondered the moral weight of various options, and considered these options in light of your hopes and ambitions, at that point, it is important to remember that you are not alone. In all likelihood, the decision you are facing is not unique. Even so, it can be easy to convince yourself that no one in the world has ever had it quite as hard as you do—or that old ways of making decisions are no longer relevant. In the two-thousand-year history of the Church, however, surely someone encountered this problem before; and he probably wrote about it. All you have to do is figure out who. Then, if you're serious about making really good decisions (and not just advantageous ones), you will have to be willing to be reformed by that person, and not just find someone who makes you feel good about yourself.

Of course, at some point in our lives, we all discover that our elders are capable of mistakes. Then comes a brief period of disillusionment, resentment, and angst during which we consider all of them idiots and begin to believe that we are enormously insightful and quite capable of making up our own minds about things regardless of what a bunch of old grumps happen to think. This is called adolescence, and if we're lucky, it doesn't last long.[5] But in the end, we, too, become parents and elders and want to help our children avoid the mistakes we made when we were their age. And so the cycle continues. A few prodigies figure this out while they are still young, but most of us have to make several wrong turns before we learn to ask for directions.

---

[5] If we're unlucky, we end up writing books with names like *Outgrowing God*, *The End of Faith*, or *God Is Not Great*.

Saint John Cassian wrote, "The Lord did not desire of himself to teach the boy Samuel [directly] through divine speech ... but he was obliged to return twice to the old man. He willed that one whom he was calling to intimate converse with himself should even be instructed by a person who had offended God, because he was an old man ... so that the humility of him who was called to a divine ministry might be tested and so that the pattern of this subjection might be offered as an example to young men."[6]

on't ask, "What would you do?"

A brother asked Father Poemen, "A legacy has been left to me. What should I do with it?"

After spending some time in silence, he said, "Return in three days, and I will tell you."

Three days later, the brother returned. "What have you decided?" he asked.

He answered, "I have decided that it is none of my business."

Asking someone what to do is futile. The person you consult surely has different priorities and a different

[6]John Cassian, *The Conferences*, trans. Boniface Ramsey (New York: Paulist Press, 1997), 98.

vocation. Instead of asking someone to decide on your behalf, ask that person, "*How* would you decide this?" Then you will be able to apply what you learn to many different decisions in the future. This is why, by and large, the Desert Fathers told stories rather than laying out rules. A story is more adaptable—it broadens your options rather than limiting them.

There's a story in Saint Thérèse of Lisieux's auto-biography about a choice she was asked to make as a child. She and her sister were offered a basket of trinkets and told to choose whatever they liked. Her older sister chose first and took a ball of wool, but Thérèse grabbed the whole basket, saying, "I choose all!" For the little saint, this summed up her whole life: "My God, *'I choose all!'* I don't want to be a *saint by halves* ... for 'I *choose all*' that You will."[7]

Saint Maximilian Kolbe told a similar story. As a ten-year-old, he had a vision of the Blessed Virgin in which she asked him to choose between a white crown and a red crown. Understanding the white to represent a life of purity and the red to represent martyrdom, he said he would take them both, thank you very much.

If sainthood is your goal, try thinking like a saint. Don't get trapped in an either/or mindset. God wants you to have everything that is good for you.

[7] Thérèse of Lisieux, *Story of a Soul: The Autobiography of St. Thérèse of Lisieux*, trans. John Clarke, O.C.D (Washington, D.C.: ICS Publications, 1996), 27.

o seek out contrary opinions.

A young philosopher went into the desert seeking wisdom and apprenticed himself for three years to a monk who did nothing but insult him. Every day, the monk would wake up, insult the philosopher, demand payment, and dismiss him. At the end of the three years, he told the young man to leave.

Thinking to himself that he had wasted his time, the philosopher headed for Athens, where he heard there was real wisdom to be learned. There he found an old bum sitting at the city gates, taunting everyone who passed. When the philosopher passed by, the old scoundrel mocked him as well. But the young man laughed.

"Why do you laugh when I taunt you?" asked the bum.

"Because I've been paying for that for three years and you just gave it to me for free."

The old man bowed low and said, "The city is yours."

Often, we make our choice first and then go looking for advice or evidence that will justify it. Psychologists call this "confirmation bias", and we do it all the time. For example, when I go out to eat, I'll pick something on the menu and then ask the waiter if it's good. But what's he going to say: "Oh that? It's disgusting. Order something else"?

Part of the problem is that we all have a tendency to think we know more than we do. It's that same tendency that keeps us from asking directions when we're lost or leads us to make confident predictions that don't come true. Doctors, ministers, politicians, actors, and scientists are particularly susceptible to this. They think that just because they know a lot about one thing, that means they know a lot about everything.

Richard Dawkins, God bless him, is a really smart guy who knows a great deal about evolutionary biology. For years, I carried his book *The Selfish Gene* around with me wherever I went. That is, until I heard him debate a creationist on the existence of God. At one point, the talk turned to evolution.

"And you have a degree in science?" Dawkins asked.

"No," answered the theologian. "Do you have a degree in theology?"

They both had a point, namely, that we'd all be a lot better off if we understood the limits of our expertise. To avoid falling into this trap, find someone who thinks you are making the wrong decision and really listen to him.

Part 3: Reflect

A young monk asked his elder, "Why is it that whenever I start working, I feel weary and disgusted, and my mind is completely empty of spiritual thoughts?"

The old monk said to him, "Because you do not really desire to pray."

For better or for worse, this is the stage where you will probably spend most time. But have you given any thought to *how* you are thinking in the first place? Interestingly, the elder in this story distinguishes between feelings, thoughts, and desires.

When confronted with a difficult decision, we are often advised, "Follow your heart." This isn't entirely bad advice. According to one of our novices, he came to us because of a coin flip. He said to himself, "Heads, I'm Dominican; tails, I'm a Benedictine." The coin came out heads, and he was disappointed, so he became a Benedictine. His story has merit precisely because he did *not* depend on the coin flip to make his decision. He let his decision be informed by his feelings, which were, to him, a mystery all the way up to the moment he saw heads. To be sure, there is value in stopping to consider how you feel about a decision, but emotions are rarely dependable guides. The heart is notoriously fickle, after all. Feelings shift with the weather. "The heart is deceitful above all things, and desperately corrupt," says the prophet Jeremiah. "Who can understand it?" (Jer 17:9). So before you follow your heart, stop to consider whether perhaps your heart may need more training before you can trust it in this matter.

So too, we are often advised to "think carefully", and this is even more important. But the intellect is not infallible either. As George Orwell supposedly said, "Some ideas are so stupid that only intellectuals believe them."[8] Folks have a way of rationalizing

---

[8] Take, for example, Nietzsche's famous saying: "That which does not kill me only makes me stronger" (which comes from a book he entitled—I kid you not—*Why I Am So Wise*). I can name twenty diseases off the top of my head that will make you weaker without killing you. And yet, folks are continually reciting this quote as though it were some earth-shattering insight.

bad decisions they've already made—or talking themselves into decisions that are utterly ruinous. What's more, if you rely exclusively on reason, you'll end up changing your mind every time you encounter a clever argument. There's an old monk of my abbey named Father Finbarr who likes to tease the junior monks when he hears them debating theology. He says, "Your argument makes a lot of sense, but I'm guessing there is someone smarter in the world with a different opinion. I'm going to believe that guy." One is tempted at first to dismiss such a statement as ridiculous. But his argument is entirely reasonable. So go ahead and make those lists of pros and cons; but understand that they aren't likely to satisfy you either, because as it turns out, the mind is almost as fickle as the heart.

What, then, do you *really desire*? In the end, we make all the greatest and most heroic decisions at a more fundamental level than the heart or the head: whom to marry, what career to pursue, how to raise our kids, whether or not to run into a burning building, whether or not to charge a machine gun nest ... For lack of a better word, I will call this level "the will". It is the will, informed—but not coerced—by intellect and emotion that should dictate the course of one's life; and the goal of life is heaven. Not all problems require the same mode of reflection. When the situation changes, you may need to change your method of decision-making.

on't just settle for the obvious answer.

Father Nistheros the Great was walking in the desert with a brother when they encountered a horrible beast. Both ran away. Disappointed, the brother said to him, "You are Nistheros the Great. What were you afraid of?"

"I was terrified," answered the old man, "that if I did not run away, you would boast to people of how brave I am."

Have you ever heard of Occam's razor? It is also called the *lex parsimoniae* (because everything sounds cooler in Latin). This problem-solving principle was formulated in the fourteenth century by a Franciscan, William of Occam, who asserted that the simplest solution was usually the right one. Translated into decision-making, it suggests that when you have two options, the simplest option is usually the best. But the really crucial word in this formulation is "usually". Complex problems sometimes have complex—or even hidden—solutions. The brother in the story above drew the obvious conclusion from Father Nistheros' behavior; but the obvious answer wasn't the right one.

o imagine what advice you would give to someone else.

Father Olympius of the Cells was tempted by lust and resolved to leave his monastery. "I guess I better get married," he thought to himself. Then, as though speaking to another, he replied, "Very well, let's give it a try." He went outside his cell and made himself a wife out of clay, and said, "Olympius, you are working for two now. Be sure you work twice as hard!"

The next morning, he made a child out of clay and said, "Look at that! Now you have a child to care for. Be sure you work a little harder to cover those expenses. And make three times as much food while you're at it." That night, he woke himself up at odd hours saying, "Your child is sick!" and "Your child just had a bad dream."

The next day, he made a second child ... and so, after a few days, he cured himself of the temptation.

Notice that Father Olympius spoke to himself "as though speaking to another". By doing so, it became clear that he had a warped view of marriage. He saw it as a quick fix for his lust problem. Thus, his "wife" would exist merely to comfort him, which was wishful thinking and selfish too. In fact, the members of his growing family had needs of their own, which he was neither prepared nor inclined to meet. Marriage was clearly not the answer to Father Olympius' crisis—such acts of desperation rarely are. By externalizing his fantasy, he was able to shed a more realistic light on it.

If you can reframe your solution in terms of the advice you might give a friend, often you will find that you gain a certain perspective you might not otherwise be aware of. For example, the answer to the question, "Would I rather play video games or do my homework?" is pretty obvious when you're just talking to yourself. When you reframe the question as though speaking to another, it sounds radically different. "Egbert, I think you should skip your homework and play video games instead" sounds like terrible advice.

Another way to do this is simply to ask the question out loud. It's easy to do and often has the effect of clarifying misconceptions and providing the sort of detachment needed to identify self-deception. This is particularly good for identifying temptations: "Should I send her an angry email?" sounds different when you announce to the room, "I'm about to send my ex-girlfriend an angry email."

STEP 3: ACT

A brother asked one of the elders, "What am I to do? I am a terrible monk. I eat too much, sleep too much, drink too much ... and I am plagued by evil thoughts."

The elder said to him, "You may do very little good, but you do it in Jesus' name. Now go back to your cell."

ou may find this hard to believe, but the happiest, holiest, most successful people are not those who make the best decisions, but those who make the best of the decisions they've already made. On a purely material level, this is why, when it comes to really weighty matters, we sign contracts, create alliances, and make promises. Sooner or later, one or the other party will want to back out. Granted, even after all this prayer and thought, we may still make the wrong decisions. But I'm afraid that is simply the consequence of being finite and fallible.

Lately, I've been hearing people talk a lot about "these uncertain times", but really, were the times ever that certain? Life is chaos, the human perspective is profoundly limited, and absolutely everything we do has eternal consequences. So how do you keep from going insane? "If I did not simply live from one moment to another," wrote Saint Thérèse of Lisieux, "it would be impossible for me to be patient; but I only look at the present, I forget the past, and I take good care not to forestall the future."[1] In the end, the secret to making a decision is simply making the decision. Because no matter what you decide, someone will make a mess of it—probably you. So take everything you've learned from this process ... and then commit to a particular course of action.

Then leave it in God's hands.

[1] Thérèse of Lisieux, *The Story of the Soul: The Autobiography of St. Thérèse of Lisieux*, trans. Rev. Thomas N. Taylor (New York: Cosimo, 2007), 175.

Part 1: Resolve

Someone asked Father Antony, "What should I do in order to please God?"

The old man replied, "Pay attention to what I tell you: whoever you may be, always have God before your eyes; whatever you do, do it according to the testimony of the holy Scriptures; in whatever place you live, do not easily leave it. Keep these three precepts and you will be saved."

I tend to pray like my father watches television, snapping from one channel to another as my attention strays. With so many distractions competing for my time, this has become a way of life. It's the way I do everything, from schoolwork to correspondence to community meetings; and I have to concede that it may be the price I pay for having instant access to limitless knowledge. If you had told me thirty years ago that you had a machine in your pocket that gave you access to all the people in the world and everything they know, I would not have believed you. Yet here we are. And while it might be worth the price of my attention span, it isn't particularly good for my prayer. The Buddhists call this state of distractibility "monkey mind", and if you want to reflect carefully and prayerfully on a single topic, you'll need to learn how to get over it.

In part, this is why monks take a vow of stability. The tradition goes all the way back to Saint Antony and his admonition that, wherever he is, a monk should stay put. His advice is startlingly simple: if you want to keep your thoughts trained on the Almighty, it is best not to keep moving around, because novelty is the enemy of concentration. It is also the enemy of good decision-making; but not for the reasons you think.

Alain de Botton, a Swiss philosopher (who happens to be an atheist, but hey, even atheists are sometimes inspired by the God in whom they profess not to believe[2]), has analyzed what makes for a successful marriage.[3] In the end, he came to this conclusion: Given

---

[2] I am indebted to my friend Father John Parker, dean of Saint Tikhon's Orthodox Seminary, for pointing this out to me.

[3] Alain de Botton, "Why You Will Marry the Wrong Person", *New York Times Sunday Review*, May 28, 2016, https://www.nytimes.com/2016/05/29/opinion/sunday/why-you-marry-the-wrong-person.html.

the odds of finding a perfect match amid the 4.5 billion people out there, you will almost assuredly marry the wrong person. And yet there are millions of happily married people in the world. How does that happen? The answer is that they commit to the marriage even though it is clearly not ideal. So in the end, de Botton concludes that commitment—sheer determination to make it work—is what distinguishes happy, successful (and I would add, holy) couples from unhappy, unsuccessful, frustrated couples. This is equally true for just about any decision you make. Nothing will ruin your dinner out like ordering the steak and thinking about the lobster for the rest of the night—and nothing will ruin the waiter's night like changing your order five times.

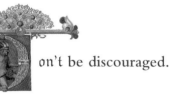 on't be discouraged.

A brother said to Father Poemen, "The Devil is attacking me, and I am very discouraged."
The old man replied, "The Devil only attacks his enemies. Be discouraged when he stops."

Just as it was Christ's vocation to die on the cross, so we may be called by God to fail from time to time. In fact, I think it's fair to say that we will all inevitably be called to fail on some level. But the Good News (with a capital G and a capital N) is that, if we can unite that failure with Christ's own suffering, it transforms into a tremendous good—not just an opportunity to grow, but a participation in the redemptive sufferings of Christ (1 Pet 4:13). Like suffering, failure can be transfigured, enriched, and elevated in the light of the Cross, which was, in its unique way, the fusion of humanity's greatest failure with its greatest victory. So do not despair. Even the wrong decision can be transformed by God to help save the world.

o keep your eyes on the prize.

Father Poemen also said, "Before a blacksmith sets to work on a project, he must decide what that project will be: a sword, a scythe, or an axe. Just so, whatever work you decide to do, first ask yourself what virtue will come of it."

As you begin a work—really, any work at all—try asking yourself, "How will I be a better person when I finish this?" Right now, I'm sitting in my hermitage writing this book on decision-making. I just ate two chocolate bars. This is literally true. They were given to me this afternoon by one of my brethren, who had been given them by one of his students. "Take these off my hands," he told me, "otherwise, I'll eat them both." I did. And I ate them both. But now, as I am sitting here with a belly full of chocolate, I'm wondering whether that was such a great idea. When I accepted the gift this afternoon, I would have done well to ask myself, "What virtue will I gain by eating two bars of chocolate?"

Mind you, a piece of chocolate every now and then does the soul good; but two full bars in a row? Had I asked myself the obvious question before beginning on that first bar, I probably would have had a bite or two, but I certainly wouldn't have said to myself, "Go ahead, Gus. What harm could it do?" Instead, I just started eating. And now I feel bloated and nauseous.

When you keep the goal in mind, not only do you find motivation for sticking with your resolution, you also avoid those things that might undermine your success.

Part 2: Relax

Twelve monks were traveling along a road at night when their guide lost the way. They knew he was lost, but he would not ask for help. Therefore, the brothers resolved to say nothing. When, the next day, the guide made excuses and apologized, they answered, "Indeed, we knew you were lost but decided it was better to remain silent rather than embarrass you."

"Truly your charity is such that you would endure death rather than speak an unkind word," he said, and he gave glory to God.

For those early monks, where they were going wasn't nearly as important as how they got there. A single unkind word would ruin the entire trip. So here's both the good news and the bad news: it doesn't really matter what you decide. If it's an easy decision, that's because you have to choose between a good option and a bad option (in which case, it's not really much of a choice, is it?); if it's a hard decision, that's because your options are all bad (in which case, you're out of luck no matter what you decide); or your options are all good (in which case, you're in luck no matter what you decide). So the pressure is off, right?

Well, not exactly. You may be too distracted to make a good decision. Your vision may be clouded by sin or vice. One of your options may be bad, and you just don't know it. One of your options may be more in line with the will of God, and you just don't know it. This is where the Desert Fathers can help; because for them, the road you're on isn't nearly as important as how you walk it. Destination and destiny are not the same thing.

on't cage the light.

Father Antony was worried about God's judgment, and prayed, saying, "Lord, why is life so unfair? Some die young and others old; some are poor and others rich; but most importantly, why are evil people so well off while good people wind up oppressed by poverty?"

A voice came to him saying, "Antony, God knows what he is doing. Mind your own business."

Gregory Treverton is a national security expert and something of a philosopher. He wrote an essay for *Smithsonian* back in 2007 called "Risks and Riddles". In this essay, he distinguished between puzzles and mysteries. A puzzle can be solved if you simply collect enough information. But a mystery, in his words, is "an attempt to define ambiguities".[3] How someone feels, for example, is a mystery. You can collect a whole bunch of medical and psychological data, but there is no guarantee that you will ever have enough information to be absolutely certain. A person's feelings may even be unknown to himself.

Possibly the hardest part about decision-making is knowing when to stop collecting data and admit that the future is a mystery, your feelings are a mystery, and God's will for you is a mystery. Virtually all of our great life decisions (and most of our small ones) are mysteries. Yet we convince ourselves that if we only had a little more information, we could guarantee the correct choice.

Father Antony's mistake wasn't that he grieved over the unfairness of the world; it was in thinking that the unfairness of the world could be explained. I've been told that Saint Augustine defined heresy as an attempt

[3] Gregory F. Treverton, "Risks and Riddles", *Smithsonian*, June 2007, https://www.smithsonianmag.com/history/risks-and-riddles-154744750/.

to cage light.[4] Don't bog yourself down trying to reduce the mystery to a puzzle; you might as well try to keep light in a cage.

D stick to the present moment.

Father Poemen said, "When you are tempted, do not be anxious about tomorrow, saying to yourself, 'How much longer will this last?' Say only, 'Today I am tempted,' and get on with your life."

Truly, the future is unknowable and the past is unchangeable, but if we heed Father Poemen's advice, we will avoid both the quicksand of anxiety and the slippery slope of false assurances. "There is not a moment," wrote Jean-Pierre de Caussade, "in which God does not present Himself under the cover of some pain to be endured, of some consolation to be enjoyed, or of some duty to be performed. All that takes place within us, around us, or through us, contains and conceals His divine action."[5] So when it comes time to

---

[4] I've also been told—and by no less a scholar than James J. O'Donnell—that he probably never said that. If you know who did, hit me up on my website.

[5] Father Jean Pierre de Caussade, S.J., trans. E.J. Strickland, *Abandonment to Divine Providence* (San Francisco: Ignatius Press, 2011), 42.

make up your mind, stick to the present moment. "Many are invited, but few are chosen," says Jesus (Mt 22:14, NAB). You *are* invited. I *am* invited. This is all that really matters.

Part 3: Revisit

Mother Sarah said, "I used to pray that everyone would like and trust me; but now I know that if everyone did, I would spend the rest of my life apologizing for letting them down. Now I just pray for a pure heart." She also said, "There is good sorrow and there is bad sorrow. Bad sorrow comes from the Devil and is weak and irrational; good sorrow comes from God and brings strength by the singing of psalms."

Even after careful prayer and reflection, you may still have made the wrong decision. In that case, you will need to back down. You will know that you have committed to the wrong decision in two ways: First, a bad decision will produce bad results. Second, a bad decision will make you feel bad.

The first way is pretty straightforward: you judge a tree by its fruit (Lk 6:43). The second way is harder to parse, because often a bad decision will feel good in the short term. It will, however, make you feel bad on a deeper level and will almost certainly produce bad results in the long term. A good decision, by contrast, might make you feel bad momentarily, but on a deeper level, you will feel a certain joy—and the long-term results will be good. For example, if you decide to drink a fifth of vodka, that is a bad decision. You might feel good at first, but the next day, you will have a terrible hangover. Furthermore, it is likely to lead to other bad decisions with the result that you wind up having to make several apologies. A good decision would be to go for a run. In the short term, you will feel bad (I've never seen a runner who looked like he was enjoying himself), but the next day, you will feel a lot better.

Yet another way to think about it is like this: Good and bad decisions are like good and bad art. Good art takes work to understand and appreciate. It is slow and difficult. It may even be frustrating at first. But it broadens your world, makes you a deeper, more interesting person, and enables you to approach life in a smarter, more nuanced way. Bad art, however, has the opposite effect. You may get a kick out of it at first, but it actually limits your imagination by presenting you with a shallow vision of what life is like.

What about big decisions, though, like quitting a job or buying property? What if you join the army and realize it just isn't the life for you; or you join the seminary and realize you aren't called to celibacy? What if you get a poodle and realize it's too smart for you? There's no sin at work here. You simply made the wrong decision. Here too you will experience good and bad results as well as good and bad feelings. But on a level that is deeper than mere feelings, you will sense that you are in the wrong place.[6] Saint Ignatius of Loyola called these deeper feelings "consolations and desolations".

on't be afraid to quit (if you have to).

They said of one of the fathers that for seven years, he asked God for a particular spiritual gift. When at last he was given it, he ran to tell one of the great elders.

"I am glad for the community, but sorry for you," said the old man, "for I am not convinced this is good for your humility."

He went back to his hermitage and prayed another seven years for God to take it back, after which he was at peace.

---

[6] Mind you, I've never met anyone who tried his vocation in a seminary or religious order who thought he had wasted his time there. I'm sure such people exist, but most ex-seminarians and ex-novices will tell you that the time they spent in discernment was a time of profound self-discovery and grace. It also looks pretty great on a résumé.

"Don't be a quitter" is only good advice if you have realistic goals. The truth is, sometimes you just have to quit.[7] You throw yourself into something and realize it isn't for you.

I have a friend who is a pediatric transplant surgeon. Her name is Aleks. One day, after an exhausting four-hour surgery, her mentor (the chief abdominal transplant surgeon at the University of Texas Medical School—a man named Steve Bynon) took her aside and said to her, "Show me your hands." She did. He turned her hands this way and that. Then he told her this story: Dr. Bynon grew up in a small town in Tennessee. When he got to college, he signed up for the swim team. He thought he had a lot of talent—that he might even make it to the Olympics. So he practiced like crazy that first year—came to practice early and stayed late. One day, the swim coach called him aside. "Steve, what are your goals here exactly?"

He said, "I want to go to the Olympics." The coach said, "Let me see your hands." The problem is, Dr. Bynon has very, very small hands. So the coach told Steve Bynon that with those tiny hands, he would never be a great swimmer—and shattered his Olympic dreams.

But that's not the end of the story. Steve Bynon went on to become one of the finest transplant

---

[7] The obvious exception is a religious or marriage vow, which is indissoluble, and irreversible, and utterly irrational. The only thing that will keep it going is trust in God.

surgeons in the world, in part because he can poke those tiny hands into very small spaces.

"Don't be a quitter!" is only good advice if your goal is realistic. Otherwise, you almost certainly need to start over with something else.

o test your assumptions.

Two old monks had lived together as brothers for many years and had never fought with one another. One monk said to the other, "Let us have a fight as other men do."

The other replied, "I do not know how."

The first one said to him, "It is easy enough. I will put a brick between us, and I will say it is mine. Then you say, 'No, it is mine,' and thus the fight will begin."

So, they put a brick between them, and the first one said, "This brick is mine."

The other said, "No, it is mine."

"If it is yours, take it," said the first monk.

So they gave up.

In 1999, a couple of geniuses in Silicon Valley developed one of the most brilliant failures of all time: the iSmell. It was a little desktop gadget that plugged into the USB port on a computer and had the capacity to reproduce thousands of smells—from flatulence to roses. But despite $20 million and major investors, it failed. Why? Because no one wants to smell the internet. Just one or two cheap prototypes might have made this clear. In the business world this is called "a lean startup". Rather than following the "build it and they will come" mindset, people who choose this approach build something small to see if anyone is interested.

Another way of testing your assumptions is to do a premortem. According to the *Harvard Business Review*, "A premortem is the hypothetical opposite of a postmortem."[8] It works like this: Before making your decision, you imagine that you have made it already—and failed. Then you work backward from that assumption to determine what led to the failure. In the case of the two old monks, they realized that fighting was simply contrary to their nature.

[8] Gary Klein, "Performing a Project Premortem", *Harvard Business Review*, September 2007, https://hbr.org/2007/09/performing-a-project-premortem.

CONCLUSION

On his deathbed, Bishop Theophilus said, "I wish I'd given this more thought."

Every monastery is a microcosm of the larger Church: there are smart monks and stupid monks and fat monks and skinny monks and diligent monks and lazy monks ... and every monastery has a crazy monk. This has been the case since the earliest days of monasticism, going all the way back to the Desert Fathers. At Saint Louis Abbey, our crazy monk was Brother Edward. And by crazy, I mean that in his room he kept invisible animals that talked to him. He was also rather a meticulous man. His utensils had to be perfectly parallel on the table before he would begin breakfast. After he died, we found that every item in his cell—every lamp, every framed photograph, every table and chair—was glued in place.

I am not meticulous. Nothing in my life is in its place. If the calefactory (that's monkish for living room) is a mess, the abbot asks me to clean it up because it was almost certainly my doing. And my brethren have taken to calling me "the late Brother Augustine" because, as my novice master once remarked, "that monk never leaves a room once."

Brother Edward was forced to sit next to me in choir for eleven years. Side by side, five times a day for eleven years, we chanted the psalms together. I remember walking past his cell one afternoon and spotting a very old copy of Ernest Hemmingway's *The Sun Also Rises* on his shelf. I asked him if I could have a look at it. He answered, "Brother Augustine, that is an autographed first edition. It will be a cold day in hell before I lend you that book." He stopped for a moment and closed his eyes as if in prayer. "In fact, it will be a cold day in hell before I lend you anything at all of any value whatsoever."

And that was that.

A few years later, the abbot decided to send me to Oxford to study theology. I may be distractible, but I'm smart. I applied and was accepted. To celebrate, and to thank the community for their patience, I prepared a festive meal, the crowning achievement of which was a chocolate walnut torte. I did this partly with Brother Edward in mind because I knew he liked his desserts. But I also did it with myself in mind, because I like chocolate.

But I did something slightly unmonkish. I made an extra torte for myself, which I cut into small pieces and froze. One larger slice I wrapped in aluminum foil and hid in the refrigerator behind the mayonnaise. The next morning, after we'd finished our morning prayers, I made myself a big cup of coffee and found a good book and a comfortable chair next to a sunny window in our library. Then I went to the refrigerator to collect my slice of torte. But when I unwrapped it, I discovered that someone had gotten to it first— indeed, had taken a bite out of my chocolate torte (I could see the tooth marks), wrapped it back up exactly as he had found it, and returned it to the refrigerator in exactly the same place.

I cannot describe for you the depths of rage that I felt at that moment, contemplating my violated, half-eaten, slobbered-on slice of chocolate walnut torte. And there was no doubt in my mind who had done it. This work of scrupulous insensitivity had Brother Edward written all over it.

I went back to the kitchen, cut another slice of torte, wrapped it in foil just like the first one, and placed it in exactly the same place in the refrigerator—but not before soaking it in Lea and Pepper's Super-Hot Cajun Pepper Sauce. The next morning, after prayers, I returned to the kitchen. There was half-chewed chocolate torte sprayed on the floor, on the refrig-erator, on the wall … It was a moment of singular triumph. A few weeks later, I left for Oxford. Brother Edward didn't even say goodbye.

When I returned to the monastery three years later, Brother Edward was on his deathbed. Cancer had rendered him comatose. But on my desk in my cell, meticulously wrapped in brown paper and tied with twine, was his autographed copy of *The Sun Also Rises*.

Sooner or later, you and everyone you know will be dead.[1] The only decision of any real consequence is: Where do you want to be after that? When you think about it—and Saint Benedict says a monk should think about it every day—no matter what we decide, we all end our lives in exactly the same place. "If we live, we live to the Lord, and if we die, we die to the Lord; so then, whether we live or whether we die, we are the Lord's" (Rom 14:8).

I'll leave you with one last saying of the Desert Fathers: An old monk was asked why he was always so joyful and never gave in to despair. "It's easy," he said. "Every morning, I wake up and remind myself that I could be dead."

Kind of takes the pressure off, doesn't it?

---

[1] "We will die," wrote Saint Francis de Sales, "and sooner than we think." *Introduction to the Devout Life* (New York: Doubleday, 1972), 60.

APPENDIX A

Decision Guide

So you have finished the book. Good for you! But let's face it: unless you actually commit to a particular course of action, this will have been little more than an academic exercise—or worse yet, a delay tactic. It's not enough just to think about the decision. At the end of the day, you have a choice to make. This worksheet is intended to help guide you through the steps of making a particular decision so that you can, in point of fact, make up your mind.

In the space below, write out the decision you are trying to make. Don't worry about the steps. Just write it out as you currently think of it.

_____

_____

_____

1. PRAY. (Write out your petition below. Ask God for help. Ask him to make you a saint.)

_____

_____

_____

Retreat. (Start by adoring him. Forget the decision for a moment and just silently listen with the ear of your heart. Write below anything that comes to you.)

_____

_____

_____

Repent. (You don't have to get too detailed here, but make a spiritual inventory of things you're not so proud of, including and especially bad decisions you've made in the past. Then try to make a more specific list of things that may be clouding your vision. Resolve to confess these sins.)

_____

_____

_____

Rebuild. (Give thanks to God for your good decisions, and thank him in advance for his help with this decision. Imagine how your life will be different, given the prayer you have made. Describe it below.)

_____

_____

_____

2. THINK. (Rewrite your decision below. Has it changed in light of your prayer?)

_____

_____

_____

Reduce. (Are you trying to make more than one decision? If so, this is the place to separate and identify them. Try rewriting your decision as if you were explaining it to a ten-year-old.)

_____

_____

_____

Refer. (Consult at least three people. Try to find a variety of opinions. Write out their advice below. Remember: don't ask them *what* they would do—ask them *how they would decide* to do it.)

_____

_____

_____

_____

Reflect. (List your options. This is the place to make your pros/cons list. Include a detailed description of how you feel about these options. What is it that you *really want?*)

_____

_____

_____

3. ACT. (Rewrite your decision below. Has it changed at all in light of your thoughts and prayers?)

_____

_____

_____

Resolve. (So? What have you decided? Write out your answer below. How do you plan to make this happen, and where in particular do you anticipate needing God's help? Choose a date somewhere in the near future—how near will depend somewhat on the type of decision you've made. Write the date below. That will be the date for second-guessing your decision.)

_____

_____

_____

Date for revisiting this decision:

Year: _____ Month: _____ Day: _____

Relax. (Now don't think about it again until the date you have chosen above. Simply live with your decision and enjoy—or suffer—the consequences. Write out below the positive and negative results of your decision. But don't judge those consequences or evaluate the decision. That will come when you revisit it. For now, just live with the results.)

_____

_____

_____

Revisit. (Ask yourself, "Have I made the right decision?" "How do I feel about where it has led me?" "What do I think about my current circumstances?" Write your answers below. You may even wish to fill out the entire worksheet once more.)

_____

_____

_____

APPENDIX B

Journal of a Decision

Man, my friends, is frail and foolish. We have all of us been told that grace is to be found in the universe. But in our human foolishness and short-sightedness we imagine divine grace to be finite. For this reason we tremble ... We tremble before making our choice in life, and after having made it again tremble in fear of having chosen wrong. But the moment comes when our eyes are opened, and we see and realize that grace is infinite. See! That which we have chosen is given us, and that which we have refused is, also and at the same time, granted us. Ay, that which we have rejected is poured upon us abundantly.

—Isak Dinesen, *Babette's Feast*

Previously published in a slightly different form in *You!* magazine and the *Buckfast Review*. Photographs are courtesy of the author.

Part I: Simple Vows

The mind cries out, explains, demonstrates, protests; but inside me a voice rises and shouts, "Be quiet mind; let us hear the heart!"

—Nikos Kazantzakis, *Report to Greco*

Galveston, Texas, 1989

March 20: What will I do with my life? I want to *BE* something! I have all this energy and don't know what to do with it. I hope I find my place sooner or later ... I've prayed for it, I've searched for it, but I can't find what I'm looking for. I have this feeling, and I don't know what to do with it. Sometimes I try to channel it into my studies, but as soon as I sit down with a book, I lose it.

Rome, Italy, 1992

April 28: Today I met some Benedictine monks. I was very impressed. I remember this girl just stared at them as they walked down the street. The policemen on their motorcycles looked downright silly next to them. I still sometimes feel that I

would like to become a priest. I would love to belong
to the Church in that way. I would love to wear those
robes! They say Vespers at 7:15. Perhaps I'll go ...

May 19: I just got a job in a monas-
tery! I can't believe it. It's such a quiet
place. I must remember to be quiet.
That will be difficult for me—a good
thing, though ... I think. I wonder if
I'll like it. This is such a foreign experience for me. I'm not used to it, but I'm sure I'll be able
to cope.

May 20: The monks keep asking me what brought me
here; well, I just don't know. Perhaps it was God ...
These guys are cool, but I could never be a monk. And
yet, living and praying and talking with them makes
me so happy ... If I were this happy all the time, who
knows how my life might turn out?

June 14: You know, I've changed a lot over the last
few years, but something has happened to me here
in this monastery that has changed me in a profound
way. Right now, I'm not too sure what it is, but I
feel as if a seed has been planted somewhere inside—
somewhere in my soul. It grows every day like
something living. It's not just confidence that I have
gained. It is something greater. I think I am beginning to feel what some people call "inner peace". The
funny thing is that it hasn't exactly made me happy.

Whatever the case, I think I am beginning to learn who I really am. It disturbs me, though, because as I learn about myself, I am more aware of what I don't know ... the more peace I find within myself, the more I am aware of the parts of me that are not peaceful. I am learning not just about myself, but about God and what he meant by creating me. I have more confidence and peace than ever before in my life—but at the same time, I am more confused and unsettled than ever before.

St. Louis, Missouri, 1995

April 11: I've been visiting this monastery, but is the monastic life really for me? I have a girlfriend! Things get so complicated. I was at peace no more than three weeks ago. Now what? Why, if I am to be a monk, would God send me a woman I could care about? A Benedictine! To spend my life in search of God! To wear the black habit! To celebrate the Eucharist, hear confessions, preach sermons! To vow my life into bonds that free my soul! To live each day in prayer, close to the heart of our Savior, close to his holy presence in the Blessed Sacrament! Am I to be a priest? Please, God, be more specific in your directions. This is a crucial moment here. Make your move, God.

April 27: I have such an awesome decision before me. I have come extremely close to entering this monastery ... but I just can't make that final leap. If I knew it was what God wanted, I would certainly trust him to work things out. But I'm just not sure ...

June 15: I'm sitting in my room wondering what I just did with my life. I walked into the monastery this morning, found the abbot, and asked him if I could join his community. I'm tired of messing around.

Very well. I'm leaving for the monastery. I'm taking a risk. I'm going for it—all out! Look, I want to do the right thing. Christ will not abandon me if I seek him honestly. I will not be a Hamlet. I'll do it—for better or for worse. On second thought, I like my life the way it is. If it ain't broke, don't fix it. I really am happy—or at least I have been. Yet all of a sudden, I feel so sad.

No, I have chosen to begin. I have chosen to stop making circles of my life and to begin the search. There comes a point when you have to move from fun to joy. Now I have to empty my heart. Now I have to put my trust—*all* my trust—in Jesus. If I seek him, he will not abandon me. Am I strong enough for this? No. Is he? Yes. He will not give me a burden I cannot carry. I can't say I know where my future lies, but I know it's time to grow up. The celibacy part is going to be tough. Really tough. And obedience ain't gonna be no cakewalk either.

June 19: My first night in the monastery. Will this be my home for the rest of my life? Oh my God. I'm scared again. I'm depressed. Can I be bound into this

monotonous cycle of living? PRAY-EAT-WORK-
PRAY-EAT-WORK-PRAY-EAT-WORK ... I'm
scared.

I'm depressed. I'm tired, too. And I want a girlfriend.

June 29: Last night I had a dream. I don't remember
the details of it, but I know that in it, I met Saint
Augustine and decided to name myself after him.
When I woke up, I pulled out his autobiography and
read the following passage: "So my two wills, one old,
the other new, one carnal, the other spiritual, were in
conflict with one another, and their discord robbed
my soul of all concentration. ... I was split between
them."[1] This is exactly what I've been going through.
But Saint Augustine gave up everything in the end.
Will I?

August 28: My first day in the habit. People call me
"Brother". The title feels strange. Like I don't deserve
it. The habit feels strange. Like I don't fit it. I don't
know whether or not I'll stay here more than a year,
but I'll try. I am not so happy as I am at peace. Does
that make sense?

St. Louis, Missouri, 1996

January 7: Tomorrow I begin my novitiate. Does it
scare me? It does. But no matter what path I choose,

---

[1] Augustine, *The Confessions* (Oxford: Oxford University Press,
2008), 140.

it will have pain. Deep, agoniz-
ing pain. If I have a girlfriend, it
might be jealousy; if I have a wife,
it might be boredom or fear for
my children. If I am celibate, it
may be loneliness. Whichever path
I choose, pain is an inevitable

consequence. Because I am human. I can't spend my
life running away from suffering.

But even God felt pain. Jesus felt pain and loneliness
and rejection. Just like me. He said that the one who
wishes to follow him must drink from the same cup as
he (Mt 20:22).

I asked for it, didn't I? "Yes," says Jesus, "yes, you
did." The cup of bitterness. The cup of loneliness. The
cup of emptiness.

January 11: I've made it through the first three days of
novitiate. So far, so good. Only 363 more days to go
(it's a leap year!). For once in my life, I have no say in
what happens to me. I am no longer in control. For one
year, I will shut up, keep my head down, and listen ...

May 29: I dreamt about surfing last night. Surfing and
having a girlfriend. I can't figure out which I miss
more. Still, I suspect I'll stick around when my novitiate is up. I am beginning to really love the silence.

June 12: What has happened over the last month?
Nothing. Everything. I have never been so busy and

so bored all at once. Nor have I ever felt so jumbled up and at peace. I'm sure that I am hard to live with.

July 4: Sometimes I pray that I am not called to be a monk. At moments like this I ask,

"Why me? Did I not have enough pain in my life that I had to go and add celibacy to my list of struggles?" I'll tell you what: nothing short of God himself will keep me in this monastery. Fortunately, I think God himself *is* keeping me in this monastery. You can consider my presence here as proof of his existence.

August 6: Perhaps I should be more open to following the Holy Spirit instead of trying to squeeze my feet into the sandals of a saint. Take it easy, Augustine. Do what you're told and follow the will of God as you feel it in your heart. You're no saint, so just work with what you've got. Amen.

August 8: Lately, my doubts have grown more serious. I told Mom and Dad I wasn't going to stay. There are other things I would like to do. Go off to L.A. Be a real writer.

August 15: Who would have thought that I would wind up in a monastery! Where will I be a year from now? Is ambition really such a bad thing? Even after fourteen months in a cloister, I still want so many worldly things. My thoughts are all questions these days . . .

August 21: How many days have I wasted away in sin? This monastery seems to have brought out the worst in me. But then, that's sort of the point, isn't it? To flush out the demons so I can meet them head-on.

My most recent demons:

Demon #1: Whining—"Why are they picking on me?"

Demon #2: Shifting the Blame—"He shouldn't have said it that way ..."

Demon #3: Tepidity—"I just do what I'm told."

Demon #4: Self-Deception—"But this is prayer for *me* ..."

Something occurred to me today. I'm a lot like the House of Israel: God singles me out, gives me this special purpose, reveals himself to me, teaches me the laws for my own sake ... and I respond by deliberately and repeatedly turning away from him. Again and again I do it. Again and again, he welcomes me back. Will I never learn?

August 24: I have been here over a year and I am still not used to waking up at five A.M. I need something to end this torturous indecision. Faith, perhaps. But since I obviously don't have enough of that, I'll ask for a miracle instead.

August 28, Feast of Saint Augustine: I had a dream this morning while I was meditating. I dreamt that I was standing in the middle of a small room. I was surrounded by snarling monsters—anthropomorphic and grotesque. They approached me on every side, poised to devour me. But instead of defending myself, I lifted my hands to heaven. And the monsters were whisked away. Weird.

October 1, Feast of Saint Thérèse of Lisieux: Over the last week, I have received three roses: a red rose, a white rose, and today, a yellow rose. What can they mean? I have made my decision. I will join the monastery.

October 8: Today, the novices had a talk with Patrick Barry, the abbot of Ampleforth. He warned us against constantly "looking over the wall". "The modern world is such a world of options," he said, "that we find it almost impossible to commit to anything. But doesn't it all boil down to trust? Isn't that the most fundamental thing expected of us?"

Someday, you will think of changing your mind, but will trust Him instead. Stick to the facts. Ignore your fantasies about the future. Picture yourself the blind man before the Pharisees: "All I know is that I was blind, and now I see" (Jn 9:25). Stop arguing with God and trust him.

November 15: What have I learned from my novitiate? That suffering is the key to real joy. Strange as it may seem, I could not find peace of mind or heart until I learned (as Saint Benedict had commanded in the Rule) to "accept humiliations joyfully." In these humiliations, I have participated in Christ's Passion.

This story is over. The end of my novitiate. The end of my beginning. As my Latin prof used to say, "Now, there's a story with a happy middle."

Part II: Solemn Vows

St. Louis, Missouri, 1997

January 1: Three days ago I took simple vows. The ceremony was beautiful, and we all cried. Now I'm a monk. I made the Brave Decision that I have always admired in others. Now I have to live it out. At least for the next three years.

January 5: I feel restless. Sometimes I get this way. Is it because I am not leading the monastic life whole-heartedly or because I'm not praying the way I should? Or is it because I belong somewhere else? If that's the case, then what exactly does "belong" mean? Surely if there is a God, he will not have allowed me to be here without a purpose. If there isn't, then none of this matters anyway. I need air.

January 12: I have not been praying enough. I've had a touch of the flu, which is an excellent excuse for sleeping through meditation—and often lectio as well—and this, I suspect, has something to do with the uneasiness and impatience that have been the soundtrack of my life of late. I do want to be a saint, but it's the daily— no, hourly—struggle of self-discipline that I find difficult. A single act of charity or kindness (even of martyrdom, perhaps) would be easier. It is the "daily grind" that gets me down. I just don't study during my study periods, pray during my prayer periods, or work during my work periods. I don't do my jobs around the monastery as well as I should (and blame others when they get frustrated), and as if my own shortcomings weren't enough to keep me occupied, I spend half my time getting angry about other people's faults.

And is prayer the solution to all this? I think it must be, because only Christ himself can free us from our sins. I almost never turn my work into prayer. What a shame to see so much good work wasted.

January 29: My first job in the monastery is sacristan. I prepare everything that will be needed for each Mass: cruets, vestments, purificators, incense ... all must be set just so. One could not design a job less suited to my temperament. It would not be an exaggeration to say that I am the worst sacristan Saint Louis Abbey has ever had. Nothing is ever in its place. Last week, I left a bowl of incense in the refectory. Father Laurence mistook it for a bowl of candy and was well into his first mouthful before he realized what he was eating. Lucky for me, he thought it was funny.

February 20: Why is it so hard to love the people I live with? Saint John says, "He who says he is in the light and hates his brother is in the darkness still" (1 Jn 2:9). Do not imagine that if you hate your brother you live in Christ and walk in the light. Well, I'm in the dark right now, and that's no joke.

February 25: Funny. I am only two months into simple vows and have already been thinking about leaving. I guess it is just in my nature to be dissatisfied with what I have. Always looking over the wall.

February 26: I was talking with my students at lunch the other day, and I began to understand what Saint Paul meant by "glorying" in his weakness. All that partying and rowdiness in college, which, objectively speaking, did me no good at all, is transformed, by virtue of my consecration to God's service, into something useful. The kids identify with it, and when it comes to giving advice, I can say, "Stay away from that. Trust me. I've been there." I feel useful. This is what happens when you confess your sins, I think. God actually draws something good out of them. Like

Saint Francis de Sales says, he turns lead to gold. I do wish, however, that pain weren't such an integral part of all this. It's not good to wish that, perhaps. Suffering, in a certain sense, is a privilege—an opportunity to share in Christ's Passion. But that doesn't mean I have to like it.

April 13: It would make more sense to me if suffering were a complete evil and man were expected to give his life for God. Instead, the Christian perspective is that suffering can be good, and God gives his life for man. What's more, God doesn't do it for the reasons we might expect: he doesn't give his life for us because we're so beautiful; he gives his life for us precisely because we are so despicable. He gives his life for our *sins*. I don't know why this makes sense to me.

I messed up all my jobs today and everyone complained. Then, to top it all off, there was no food left when I showed up for dinner, and I got in trouble for making myself a sandwich. Why am I here? Why am I doing this to myself? Am I ambitious? Ambitious for what? Heaven? Bah! I've got everything so jumbled up inside, and the irony of it all is that when people see this "young monk" they imagine that I must be floating on a cloud of peace. They don't see the ripping loneliness. They don't see my sins, my lusts, my cruelty ... All they see is the happy monk.

And yet ... and yet ... though I hate to admit it when I'm in one of these moods ... there is, underneath it all, a certain deeper sense of joy.

But I'm in a bad mood and I don't want to talk about it.

June 26: Well, I made it through my second (or is that the third? fourth?) vocation crisis; and, as might be expected, I feel stronger than ever. It is a quiet Sunday afternoon. I have some time to myself, so I am sitting on the back porch of the monastery with a cup of coffee and some Oreos to watch a storm roll in. Storms remind me of fear without actually frightening me, which is why I like them so much. Floods of thunder sing the story. In God's temple, we all cry Glory! (Ps 29:9)

Aja Marie Spalding Photography. Used with permission.

September 4: I'm getting a little tired of being a monk. Father Luke says that's a good sign because it means I'm starting to really be a monk. Right. It's a no-win situation, if you think about it. Or a no-lose situation. This morning, coincidentally, I read a little excerpt from the autobiography of Thérèse of Lisieux. Her sister Celine had lost her desire to become a nun on the eve of her first profession. "That's perfect," the little saint told her. "Now you are ready to take vows. It's a temptation from Satan." See what I mean? You just can't win.

September 12: This morning after Mass, a man in his fifties walked up to me outside of our church and took my hand. It surprised me. "You're doing a good thing here," he said. "Stick with it. And remember: no matter how hard it gets, it's not as hard as marriage." He started to walk away, then turned and came back. "I was in the seminary for two years," he said. "I left because I didn't think I could handle the celibacy. Then I got married and found out I could!" He winked at me and walked back to his car. His wife was waiting for him. Maybe the grass isn't so green on the other side. Nonetheless, I'll bet I don't stick it out in this monastery. My guess is that I'll leave when my simple vows run out. Perhaps I'll go off to New York. Try to become a real writer.

December 22: All of life is conflict: interior, exterior, relational, vocational, intellectual … Sometimes, I just don't feel strong enough to keep fighting—or even to keep fighting the fighting. There is something to be said for abandonment to Divine Providence.

Brother Basil and I seem always to be at odds. We even fought over the heater in the car. Brother Martin hates my guts. Father Paul and Father Luke think I'm egocentric, and they're probably right. Is there a way to move with this?

Enough of me. This is God's day. Advent. I am waiting for the Incarnation.

1998

January 7: I do have a good life. It has some suffering, some sorrow ... but it has purpose. And I do the things I love on a daily basis. Sometimes I doubt if I'll make it as a monk. But tonight I don't.

March 7: I forgot to return the car keys again today. Everyone got on my case. It's not easy living with twenty-five other guys. Sometimes I feel like they're driving me crazy. But you know, it's really just I who am driving me crazy. Dorotheos of Gaza says that if a brother annoys you, then it is your own fault. You are like "winter wheat"—outwardly calm, but inwardly empty. He's right. I can afford to be patient with my own shortcomings.

Sure, it would be nice if we all had the same faults. That way, when I'd lose the keys to the car, everyone would understand. But of course, we'd never drive anywhere.

April 15

A Prayer at the End of the Day

Lord, I made a few mistakes today. But I have also accomplished a few small things as well. I prayed. I worked. I tried to conform my life to your will (whatever that is). And ultimately, the trying is the most important part. I thank you for the privilege of being alive and the honor of being your servant. These alone are all the consolation I need. Thank you for your many gifts to me. You are indeed great. Tomorrow, I will try again.

 June 27: At a retreat last weekend, an old lady told me I reminded her of Saint Francis. That amuses me for a number of reasons. First of all, how could she possibly know what Saint Francis was like? What she must have meant was that I reminded her of the qualities she imagines Saint Francis might have had. So what are those, I wonder? When I think of Saint Francis, I imagine a sort of happy-go-lucky, fly-by the-seat-of-your-pants kind of hippie. I think of someone who has perfected a certain sense of joyful peace, abandonment to Providence, and childlike trust in God. But from my perspective, none of that fits me.

Could it be that other people see me differently than I really am? If truth be told, I'm a class-A worrier. That doesn't seem to fit with the image I have of Saint Francis. And yet saints are complex characters, aren't they? Could Saint Francis have been a worrier? That would imply a lack of trust in God. But when God called, Francis didn't hesitate. Of course, if a crucifix spoke to me, I guess I wouldn't hesitate either. More likely, I'd check myself into a hospital.

I've been having second thoughts about my vocation for two years now. Am I just wasting my time? Lord, make me an instrument of your peace.

July 2: Most of the time, I just feel frustrated when I'm praying, but every now and then, a little shaft of light pierces the darkness. Hands clasped before my face, thumbnails touching my nose, I search the air in front of me, invisible as God (and just as present). Then I hear him: "This is where you belong," says the Silence, "just like this. This is your job."

July 9: I tell the kids in our school that monks are the spiritual Navy SEALS of the Catholic Church. Today we took another casualty. Father Jonah informed us that he is leaving the community—and the priesthood. In a community of only twenty-five, that's a big upset. Well, you can't fight a battle without casualties, I suppose. And we're on the front lines. Still ... it's so sad. At times like this, the community is, in fact, unusually graced. Father Abbot had a chapter meeting of all the monks, and it was a beautiful thing to see them bind together. Our little differences, our petty quarrels, seem so insignificant in the face of a lost vocation.

Father Abbot asked me in private if all this had led me to question my own vocation. On the contrary, I feel all the stronger. I say to myself, "By God, I won't let that happen to me! The world needs monks and the world needs me!"

August 16: As I approach my last year in simple vows, I ask myself again, "Is this for me?" While the thought of a lifelong commitment scares me, the thought of leaving saddens me. Which is worse: being scared or being sad?

November 1: Here I am a monk—an "icon of Christ at prayer"—and yet I skip prayers whenever I can. Sometimes, it's as though I would rather do anything than pray: read a book, floss my teeth, wash my socks ...

November 27: I am still plowing through my daily prayers. Often they are a joy. Most of the time, it's just work. *Ora et Labora* (Prayer and Work) is the Benedictine motto. It ought to be *Ora Est Labora* (Prayer *Is* Work).

Brother Basil will take simple vows in January, right about the same time as Michael will be joining the postulancy. Brother Basil, Brother Michael, and I seem to be sticking it out, so our little monastery continues to grow. We have filled up all the cells now, and monks are living in the guest quarters. Praise God.

1999

October 10: I've been so busy the past few months, I've hardly had time to write: teaching, coaching, running the kitchen, seminary ... and solemn vows are just around the corner! Have I thought this out properly? I told the abbot I wanted to take vows, but did I mean it?

October 25: So. The religious life. IS THIS WHAT I REALLY WANT?!?! Two months from solemn vows and I can honestly say ... I don't know. Some days I like doing this, and some days I don't. What is all this anger and loneliness about? Who am I? What does God want me to be? For three years I've been wrestling with this decision. I would ask God directly if I thought he'd give me a straight answer.

Lord, you know how I have agonized over this decision. Grant, then, that this, my final resolve, might be nothing more or less than the fulfilment of your holy will. I can't take vows any more than I can live them out faithfully. But in you, all things are possible. So I pray that you will grant me today the great gift of perseverance (and while you're at it, throw in patience and chastity and prudence and wisdom and self-abasement so that I might be less of a burden to my brothers).

Lord, grant that I may ever live through you and in you.

November 8: Can't I put this decision off? It's not like the monastery is going to move away. I could spend a year or two on my own. Date around a little more. Do some more writing. Maybe do grad school.

 The real issue here is trust, isn't it? I guess when push comes to shove, I just don't trust God. Or maybe I don't really believe that he exists. Would he allow me to take a vow I couldn't keep? Would he let me do something that would make me lonely for life? If that's the price of heaven, then heaven had better be good. Lord, can I trust you? Just prove to me that you exist. Give me a sign. I need proof.

Dear Augustine,

You need proof? Has not your whole life been a testament to my trustworthiness? Have you forgotten how lucky you are? Where do you think all this comes from? Were you there when I set the stars in the sky? Were you there when I pulled earth from the sea? Were you there when I punched a hole in the darkness and brought forth light?

You get back to work. Let me worry about proof and trust.

— God

November 20: This morning, the community voted on whether or not I should be allowed to take solemn vows. They decided that I should. There is only one more step to take, then: the vows themselves.

Simple vows were easy enough, but solemn vows are a whole different story. I imagine myself growing old here. Dying here. It scares the bejeebers out of me. How can I make a commitment like this? Once those vows are taken ... man, that's it! No more women. Period. No wife. No children.

It's settled, then. I am incapable of following through on a commitment like this. So why do I still want to take vows? I guess it all boils down to trust, again. Do I trust God enough to throw my life in his hands?

I guess I do.

I mean, where else would I go?

December 4: Outside, the rain is whispering against the window of my cell. I am lonely. On my desk sit three hundred invitations to my solemn profession. So it is settled. I am to be a monk. What a struggle, though. I do want to be a saint. Honest. But why can't it be easy? I have the potential. We all do, right? So why can't I pull it off? Lord, save me from myself.

I'm scared, too. In a month, I will take solemn vows. What makes me think I can make a commitment like that? I can't even take responsibility for the car keys! How am I going to take responsibility for this? How am I going to make it fifty years? I barely made it through the last four! In a sense, outright martyrdom would be easier. (Not entirely out of the question ... they already blame Catholics for all the world's social ills—overpopulation, environmental abuse, misogyny, racism, war ...). At least it would be over quickly.

On the other hand, you only live once.

December 27: I told Father Paul after dinner tonight that I was scared to take vows. He said, "That's because you're focused on what you are giving God, and not what God will be giving you. Our Lord is never outdone in generosity."

"All right then," I said to him. "What's in it for me?"

"Are you familiar with computer terminology?" he asked.

"A bit," I answered, wondering where this conversation was going.

"Your solemn vows are like a baptismal upgrade. The grace you received at baptism will be renewed, refreshed, expanded, fortified ..."

That makes sense to me.

December 31: The night before. I can't believe it has come to this. I will make my solemn vows tomorrow. SOLEMN VOWS! There's no backing out now.

Vows.

The concept is just too big. I can't wrap my mind around it. Every now and then, the full weight of my decision hits home, and I feel nauseous. By far and away, this is the most frightening thing I have ever done. Ten years ago, when I was on beach patrol, someone spotted a corpse floating next to the pier near my tower. I had to wade into the water to look for it. That was scary. But not as scary as this.

2000

January 1: It is finished. At nine A.M., I became the first monk of the millennium! On the way over to church, Brother Aidan looked across the hall at me and said, "I can't believe you're doing this!" I can't believe I did it. God, I hope I don't regret this. I feel like I ought to be depressed. Perhaps I am depressed. Do I regret what I have done? Was I really ready for the commitment? I don't know. But who ever is? I certainly wouldn't get this much preparation for marriage. And I don't plan on making it by my own strength anyway. I'm going to let Jesus take over from here on out. And why not, huh? I have no choice now.

January 3: At last I am in solemn vows. I am a monk. I shall always be a monk. I shall die a monk. At last I can say with complete confidence that I have a vocation to the monastic life. I have  found my place in the world. My entire life is consecrated to Jesus Christ. From now on, everything I do is consecrated to Christ: I wake for Christ, I sleep for

Christ, I work and play and teach and learn for Christ. I eat cereal for Christ, brush my teeth for Christ, lose the car keys and annoy the brethren for Christ. I live for Christ.

Laus tibi Domine.

RESOURCES

If you would like to dig a little deeper, here are some sources I recommend. I relied pretty heavily on them myself.

Barron, Robert. *How to Discern God's Will for Your Life.* Skokie, IL: Word on Fire Catholic Ministries, 2016.

Calloway, D.H. *No Turning Back: A Witness to Mercy.* Stockbridge, MA: Marian Press, 2018.

de Caussade, Jean-Pierre. *Abandonment to Divine Providence.* Translated by E.J. Strickland. St. Louis: B. Herder Book Company, 1921.

Duhigg, Charles. *The Power of Habit: Why We Do What We Do in Life and Business.* New York: Random House Trade Paperbacks, 2014.

Eden, D. *The Thrill of the Chaste: Finding Fulfillment While Keeping Your Clothes On.* Notre Dame, IN: Ave Maria Press, 2015.

Gallagher, Timothy M. *Discerning the Will of God: An Ignatian Guide to Christian Decision Making.* New York: Crossroad Publishing Company, 2018.

Heath, Chip, and Dan Heath. *Decisive: How to Make Better Choices in Life and Work.* London: Random House Business, 2014.

Kahneman, Daniel. *Thinking, Fast and Slow.* New York: Farrar, Straus and Giroux, 2013.

Scanlan, Michael, and James D. Manney. *What Does God Want?: A Practical Guide to Making Decisions.* Manchester, NH: Sophia Institute Press, 2018.

Thaler, Richard H., and Cass R. Sunstein. *Nudge: Improving Decisions about Health, Wealth and Happiness.* London: Allen Lane, 2021.

The Sayings of the Desert Fathers: The Alphabetical Collection. Kalamazoo, MI: Cistercian Publications, 2004.

Ward, Benedicta, and Norman Russell. *The Lives of the Desert Fathers.* Piscataway: Gorgias Press, 2009.

Wortley, John. *The Book of the Elders: Sayings of the Desert Fathers; the Systematic Collection.* Collegeville, MN: Cistercian Publications, 2018.

Wortley, John, and Samuel Rubenson. *More Sayings of the Desert Fathers: An English Translation and Notes.* Cambridge; New York; Port Melbourn; New Delhi; Singapore: Cambridge University Press, 2019.

ILLUSTRATION SOURCES

All of the illustrations inside this book were created by the author using art found on the internet. These sources are listed below by page number, and most of them are in the public domain. The link to the Creative Commons License, being provided per usage agreement, is https://creativecommons.org/licenses/by-sa/4.0/deed.en. The works protected by this license have been altered by the author.

9   José Luiz Bernardes Ribeiro. *Communion of Saints.*
     Giusto de' Menabuoi, *Paradise* (detail). Baptistry, Padua.
     Wikimedia Commons. Creative Commons License.
     Portraits of friends and associates are courtesy of the
     author.

11 Jakec. *Two Roads Diverged in a Wood ...* Wikimedia Commons. Creative Commons License.

Peter Christus. *Portrait d'un Chartreux.* Metropolitan Museum of Art, New York. Wikipedia.

15 U.S. Government Photographer. *Yalta Conference.* National Archives and Records Administration, College Park, Maryland. Wikipedia.

Eduard von Grützner. *Beschauliche Ruhe.* Dorotheum. Wikimedia Commons.

18 Grant Wood. *American Gothic.* Art Institute of Chicago. Wikipedia.

21 Charles C. Ebbets. *Lunch atop a Skyscraper.* Bettmann Archive. Wikipedia.

Pittore Lombardo. *Ritratto di un frate francescano.* Accademia Carrara, Bergamo, Italy.

23 *Detail of a Miniature of the Author Writing His Book.* British Library Catalogue of Illuminated Manuscripts.

25 Nicolas Régnier. *Self-portrait with an Easel.* Harvard Art Museums. Wikimedia Commons. This image is repeated on pages 45 and 67.

Portrait of a Monk in Prayer. Metropolitan Museum of Art, New York.

29 Emanuel Leutze. *Washington Crossing the Delaware: On the Evening of Dec 25th. 1776, Previous to the Battle of Trenton.* Metropolitan Museum of Art, New York. Wikimedia Commons.

Francesco Guarino. *St Anthony Abbot and the Centaur.* Photograph courtesy of Sotheby's, 2021.

31 Freeman Gage Delamotte. *Illuminated Letter "D" within a Decorated Border.* Metropolitan Museum of Art, New York. Wikimedia Commons. This image is repeated throughout the work.

   Detail of a Miniature of a Demon. British Library Catalogue of Illuminated Manuscripts.

32 *Miniature of Saint Odo of Cluny.* Wikimedia Commons.

34 Cassius Marcellus Coolidge. *A Friend in Need.* Wikimedia Commons.

   Jacopo de' Barbari. *Portrait of Fra Luca Pacioli with a Student.* National Museum of Capodimonte, Naples, Italy. Wikimedia Commons.

36 Hieronymus Bosch. *Anthony with Monsters.* Van Lanschot Collection. Wikimedia Commons.

37 *Author at Writing Desk.* National Library of Wales. Wikimedia Commons.

39 Stanley Spencer. *Shipbuilding on the Clyde: Bending the Keel Plate.* Imperial War Museums, United Kingdom. Wikimedia Commons.

   Spinello Aretino. *Exorcism of St. Benedict.* San Miniato al Monte, Florence, Italy. Wikimedia Commons.

41 Cenni di Francesco di Ser Cenni, *Incoronazione della Vergine con Sannti, Tentazioni di sant'antonio.* J. Paul Getty Museum, Los Angeles, California. Photograph by Sailko. Wikimedia Commons. GNU Free Documentation License. Image repeated on pages 71 and 75.

42 *Marginal Painting of a Friar with a Musical Instrument and a Woman Dancing from the Maastricht Hours.* British Library.

45 Sofonisba Anguissola. *Portrait of a Monk*. Private Collection. Wikimedia Commons.

48 Georges Seurat. *A Sunday on La Grande Jatte*. Art Institute of Chicago. Wikimedia Commons.

Il Sodoma (Giovanni Antonio Bazzi). *Life of St Benedict: How Benedict Brings Back a Hook*. Territorial Abbey of Monte Oliveto Maggiore. Wikimedia Commons.

50 *Detail of a Devil from the Taymouth Hours*. British Library.

52 Il Sodoma (Giovanni Antonio Bazzi). *Life of St Benedict: Benedict Founds Twelve Monasteries*. Territorial Abbey of Monte Oliveto Maggiore. Wikimedia Commons. Image also appears on page 83.

55 James McNeill Whistler. *Arrangement in Grey and Black No. 1 (Portrait of the Artist's Mother, Whistler's Mother)*, Musée d'Orsay, Paris. Wikipedia.

Juan Andrés Ricci de Guevara. *Portrait of a Benedictine Monk*. Private Collection. Wikimedia Commons.

57 *Satan Tempting Christ to Change Stones into Bread*. Bibliothèque Municipale, Besançon, France. "Lent—Temptations in the Wilderness—Clever Devil Turns Stones into Bread". *It's about Time* (blog).

59 Lorenzo Monaco. *Benedikt Erweckt den Kleinen Klosterbruder zum Leben*. Uffizi Gallery, Florence, Italy. Photograph from Yorck Project. Wikimedia Commons.

61 George Peter Alexander Healey. *The Peacemakers*. White House, Washington, D.C. Wikimedia Commons.

Il Sodoma (Giovanni Antonio Bazzi). *Life of St Benedict: How Benedict Unties a Peasant.* Territorial Abbey of Monte Oliveto Maggiore. Wikimedia Commons.

64 *Detail of a Miniature of the First Temptation of Christ from a Psalter.* British Library.

65 Il Sodoma (Giovanni Antonio Bazzi). *Life of St Benedict: Benedict Is Tempted.* Territorial Abbey of Monte Oliveto Maggiore. Wikimedia Commons. Image also appears on pages 74 and 121.

67 Juan Rizi. *La Cena de San Benito.* Museo del Prado, Madrid. Wikimedia Commons. Image also appears on page 79.

69 Jan Van Eyck. *The Arnolfini Portrait.* National Gallery, London. Photographed by Gennadii Saus i Segura. Wikimedia Commons. Creative Commons License.

Jacopo de' Barbari, *Portrait of Fra Luca Pacioli with a Student.* National Museum of Capodimonte, Naples, Italy. Wikimedia Commons.

72 Guillaume de Diguleville, *Pèlerinage de la vie humaine.* British Library.

74 Edward Hopper. *Nighthawks.* Art Institute of Chicago.

77 Saint-Omer of Thérouanne. *Detail of Marginal Image of a Monk Holding Prayerbook and a Woman's Torso behind Him.* British Library Catalogue of Illuminated Manuscripts.

79 Paul Delaroche. *Napoléon Bonaparte Abdicated in Fontainebleau.* Museum der bildende Künste, Leipzig, Germany. Wikidata.

81 Master of the Ingeborg Psalter. *Initial D: The Fool with Two Demons* (detail). J. Paul Getty Museum, Los Angeles, California.

85 Winslow Homer. *The Gulf Stream*. Metropolitan Museum of Art, New York.

Domenico Veneziano. *The Stigmatization of St. Francis*. National Gallery of Art, Washington, D.C. Wikimedia Commons.

89 *St. Gall and His Companion Bear*. Abbey Library of St. Gallen, Switzerland. Used with permission.

95 Michelangelo Merisi da Caravaggio. *The Calling of Saint Matthew*. Contarelli Chapel, Church of San Luigi dei Francesi, Rome. Wikimedia Commons.

121 Raffaello Sanzio da Urbino. *The School of Athens*. Vatican Museums. Wikipedia.

Il Sodoma (Giovanni Antonio Bazzi). *Life of St Benedict: Benedict Drives a Devil Out of a Stone* and *Benedict Discovers Totila*. Territorial Abbey of Monte Oliveto Maggiore. Wikimedia Commons.

123 Sandro Botticelli. *Birth of Venus*. Uffizi Gallery, Florence, Italy. Google Art Project. Wikimedia Commons.

Anthony van Dyck. *The Infanta Isabella Clara Eugenia*. Walker Art Gallery, Liverpool, England. Wikimedia Commons.